The Social Leadership Handbook

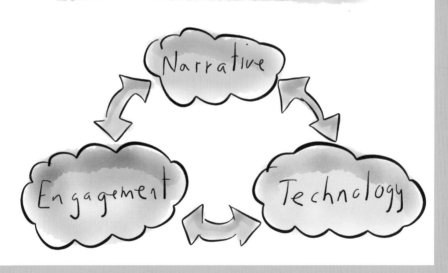

Narrative

Engagement

Technology

by

Julian Stodd

Printed in the United Kingdom
The Printing House
London | Chester

Design & Typesetting
SWATT Design Ltd.

First Printing, 2014

ISBN 978-0-9573199-6-7

SeaSalt Learning

www.julianstodd.wordpress.com
seasaltlearning.com

Table of Contents

Part 3: Application 80

Summary 97

The Social Leadership Handbook

Prologue

Let's start with the end in mind: Social Leadership encapsulates the mindset and skills required to be an effective leader in the Social Age. It recognises that power and authority are founded more on what you share and how you build your reputation than simple positional authority. It's a model of leadership that is more fluid and relevant than those based on longevity, situation or hierarchy. Under a social model, sharing and narrating trump command and control. It's a collaborative venture with community at it's heart.

The NET Model of Social Leadership is built around three Dimensions: 'Narrative', 'Engagement' and 'Technology'.

Each of these Dimensions is made up of three components, comprising the skills, concepts, models and attitudes of the Social Leader. The NET model is both an idea and a call to arms.

This book is a guide for organisations looking to develop Social Leadership and for individuals looking to become Social Leaders.

The NET Model of Social Leadership is not intended to replace other models of leadership: it's complimentary. It works in both formal and social spaces, recognising that, in the Social Age, we have to develop authority in both to be effective.

Being a Social Leader is about agility and fluidity of role: it's highly contextual and can complement other styles. At heart, it's anchored in the principles and ethics of value led behaviour: it's about authenticity and support. You can't be a Social Leader all alone.

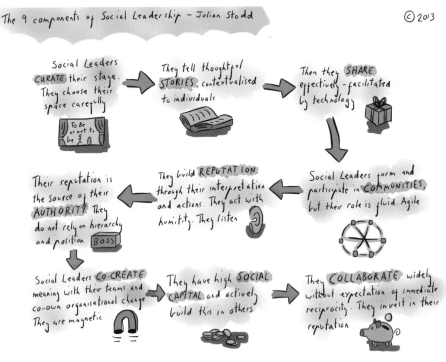

The 9 components of Social Leadership – Julian Stodd © 2013

Social Leaders CURATE their stage. They choose their space carefully

To Be or not to be

They tell thoughtful STORIES, contextualised to individuals

Then they SHARE effectively - facilitated by technology

Social Leaders form and participate in COMMUNITIES, but their role is fluid. Agile

They build REPUTATION. through their interpretation and actions. They act with humility. They listen

Their reputation is the source of their AUTHORITY. They do not rely on hierarchy and position BOSS

Social Leaders CO-CREATE meaning with their teams and co-own organisational change. They are magnetic

They have high SOCIAL CAPITAL and actively build this in others

They COLLABORATE widely without expectation of immediate reciprocity. They invest in their reputation

The 9 components of social leadership outlines a journey through the skills and mindset needed to be truly agile

The first Dimension of Social Leadership is 'Narrative': this is about 'curation', 'storytelling' and 'sharing'. It's about you, yourself, inward looking, taking a stance and thinking about how you position yourself in your environment. It's about finding things out, finding the meaning in it and sharing it with relevant people, adding value as you do so. It's about being part of the conversation instead of part of the noise. Whilst socially collaborative technologies allow us to share easily, so much of what is shared, copied and re-blogged is simply noise. To be effective, Social Leaders cut through the noise with relevance and clarity.

So Narrative is about:

CURATION - Finding things out and determining what's valid from what's just noise. It's about identifying networks and communities and seeing where the nodes and amplifiers sit. It's about quality and coherence, not volume and mass.

STORYTELLING - Do you know how to identify the narrative that sits under the story? Can you find the meaning? Social Leaders need to be able to take their curated ideas and knowledge and forge coherent narratives, then flesh them out into stories that are relevant and timely to the audience. It's about understanding how stories are told and retold, so although the individual words change, the narrative is constant.

SHARING - This is a core skill of the Social Age. Curating content, finding the meaning and then sharing the stories effectively. This may involve technology, but it's not purely that. It's a mindset to share that counts: recognising that knowledge in itself is no longer enough.

In summary, Narrative is about **curating knowledge**, *finding the* **meaning** *within it,* **forming stories** *and understanding how to* **share** *and* **amplify** *these. Narrative skills form the heart of personal effectiveness for Social Leaders.*

Following on from 'Narrative' is 'Engagement'. Engagement is about:

COMMUNITY - Social Leaders operate in communities: both formal and informal spaces where meaning is created. With 'Narrative', we looked at how to be an effective storyteller, with 'Engagement' we are looking at the spaces in which those stories are told and how to use them to build your reputation and authority. This is about understanding why people engage in communities and how we can both form and sustain them effectively.

REPUTATION - As we move beyond purely hierarchical forms of power and authority, we enter the reputation economy. Reputation forms the engine of our effectiveness. If our reputation is weak, even if our stories are strong, we will struggle to get them heard or amplified. Reputation is forged in communities, founded on the quality of our stories and effectiveness of our sharing. Reputation can transfer from social to formal environments.

AUTHORITY - Authority is born from reputation, based on the stories we curate. Authority in the social age is fluid, not fixed in bricks and mortar, and may be contextual. This component of Social Leadership is about recognising when authority is exercised and how, about becoming magnetic.

In summary, Engagement is about understanding the **shape** *and* **structure** *of informal and formal* **communities***, understanding* **how and why people come together** *to work and learn. Reputation is the engine that powers our* **effectiveness***: it's based on* **actions***, not* **hierarchy***, and authority is the outcome. We seek authority as leaders, but it's based on everything we've seen so far: curating knowledge, finding meaning, telling stories and understanding the ecosystem they exist in.*

Following 'Engagement' comes 'Technology'. This isn't about circuit boards and operating systems, it's about social collaboration, fairness and reach.

CO-CREATION is the process by which meaning is created within communities and the way in which culture changes over time. I use a seven stage model of co-creation, often taking place within scaffolded social learning environments. Co-creation is the sense making process. Co-creation and the co-ownership of change are core concepts for the Social

Age. Relevant to this are notions of the three levels of narrative: personal, co-created in groups and organisational.

SOCIAL CAPITAL is one's ability to survive and thrive in these spaces. Effective social leaders have high social capital and develop it in others. This generosity and humility reinforces reputation and authority. It's about keeping the field level and ensuring fairness and equality for all.

COLLABORATION is what it's all about: coming together and creating meaning, beyond that which we can do alone. Social Leaders collaborate widely: they engage in relationships without an expectation of immediate reciprocity. In time, all things balance out.The quality of how Social Leaders collaborate is what makes them effective and respected.

*In summary, Technology is about **socially collaborative conversations**, about the **co-creation of meaning** in communities, about supporting **engagement** and **development** in these communities and about **collaborating**, to achieve more than we ever can alone.*

The NET model of social leadership is a circle, because we keep moving around it. It's what keeps us agile!

The full NET Model can be represented in a circle: we start with 'curation'
and end up at 'collaboration'. The circle represents an agile journey through:
once we have mastered the skills, we continue to refine them.

Introduction

Introduction

This is a book about Social Leadership: a style of leadership that bridges the gap between the formal organisational space and semi formal social ones. It's not an alternative to other leadership styles, it's complimentary. And it's essential for any individual or organisation that wants to remain agile, to remain relevant in the Social Age.

Consider this a first draft: I've been developing the ideas here over the last year as part of a wider exploration of the ecosystem of the Social Age, a time when change is constant and the very nature of work is evolving. Social Leadership is one part of that change, you can read about other elements on my blog here www.julianstodd.wordpress.com.

I say it's a first draft because life and learning, in the Social Age, is in constant beta. What we know today will get us to tomorrow, but we'll have to learn more again tomorrow to keep ahead. The ideas and practices I present here are for today: in time, the ecosystem will develop further and they will need updating. Welcome to the Social Age, where change is constant and we live in constant beta.

In the first part of this Handbook, i'm going to explore the foundations for Social Leadership. This involves defining the Social Age, looking at the concept of '*Socially Collaborative Technology*' and understanding how Social Leadership is based within communities and the reputation that they support. We will explore how social styles subvert more formal leadership approaches and why Social Leadership is contextual, consensual and based on humility.

The second half of the Handbook is an exploration of the NET Model in detail: this is a structured curriculum based around three dimensions and nine separate skills that social leaders need to develop to be truly effective.

The Social Age

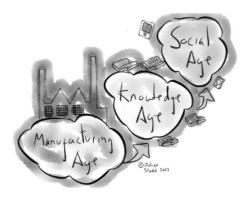

The manufacturing Age to the Social Age: although a simplification, it represents the shift to a connected, liberally communicative world.

I use the term *'The Social Age'* to talk about the environment we inhabit today: it's a time when the very nature of work is evolving, changing to reflect a revised social contract and the advancement of technology to facilitate sharing and community.

In the Manufacturing Age, we used to make stuff: banging together lumps of iron, burning coal, wrestling value from the very earth itself as we wrought iron and carved railways through the landscape, smelting and mining, until we outsourced it all and specialised production in a global network of trade and exchange, bringing us to the Knowledge Age. We convinced ourselves that this was ok: we no longer made stuff, but we had the knowledge, we did the clever bit ourselves and the knowledge was what really mattered.

But then the internet evolved and Google was born, phones got smart and small and our relationship with knowledge changed. Finding stuff out is easy. Making sense of it is what counts. Welcome to the Social Age.

Power and authority, that used to be gained through knowledge alone, is now based more in effectiveness, in being able to create value and meaning through the effective use of knowledge and resources in agile ways. Simply knowing stuff is not enough. Business models used to be based on hiding knowledge away, portioning it out behind paywalls and gateways, compartmentalising it, hiding it in books and charging for access. Free became the new way to add value and sharing became the differentiating behaviour. Why? Because the value of knowledge alone is driving down to zero.

I recently gave a guest lecture at Dublin City University for the Masters course on *'Creating effective learning in the Social Age'*. It was a broad presentation, starting with how we communicate using stories, progressing to an exploration of a methodology for learning, journeying through mobile technology and social learning and ending up with some pragmatic steps for creating effective learning solutions.

The questions from the group were many and varied, reinforcing for me the value in taking time out to just think about how we communicate, how we learn. The thought that carried me through was that here we are, in the Social Age, even though many organisations haven't realised it yet.

As I heard stories of sectors trying to control and reject seml formal spaces and resources, trying to restrict technology, trying to own the conversation, it made me realise just how far behind the times they are. Whilst, on the one hand, we see traditionally conservative industries such as Finance or Healthcare starting to experiment in pockets with innovative social learning and leadership approaches, there are, still many bastions of resistance, who fail to see that the walls are crumbling around them.

Everything about how we work and play is changing. The fundamental structure of our society is evolving. How we communicate and, indeed, how we think, is in flux.

We are not at the dawn of the Social Age: we are already here and we're kicking down the walls!

We are in the Social Age of learning. Formal hierarchies count for less than our social communities an ability to create meaning.

The Social Age is about high levels of engagement through informal, socially collaborative technology. It supports agility by allowing many and varied connections and the rapid iteration of ideas in communities that are 'sense making'.

The notion of 'sense making' is worth exploring further: it's about how communities iterate ideas, each member bringing their own perspective and interpretation and, collectively, find the meaning. A large part of the power of the Social Age comes through the way that we operate within and alongside multiple communities, each of which may specialise or be generalist, but all contributing to this collective sense making capacity. Our communities literally make us more effective than we can ever be in isolation.

'Sense making' is the activity we carry out in our communities: it's where we find the meaning.

Social Learning and Leadership approaches subvert formal hierarchy because they are powered by reputation, not formal status or longevity in role. Learning is extended and expanded as it moves beyond the purely classroom based environment and into performance support and real world application. In this context, learning is more directly owned by the individual and is highly portable: instead of existing in abstract, formal classrooms, it exists where you work.

Social Learning can be viewed as the semI formal layers that surround the formal, the conversations that take place around it. It's the communities of learners who create meaning, rather than accepting what they are told without question. Social Learning is a mindset to rebel, to reach out and seek expertise and be unafraid to ask *'why?'*.

In this context, the role of the Social Leader is based on facilitation, mentoring and coaching rather than grounded in knowledge or formal hierarchy, both of which have diminished status. The skill is in creating communities of change, forming and working within these *'sense making'* groups.

Technology facilitates the experience, it facilitates learning, but it doesn't guarantee it. The Social Age couldn't exist without it. It's the quality of stories we tell and the relevance to the individual that counts and today that relevance may be wider than simply their current job. As the fundamental bond of trust between employer and employee breaks down, as the notion of a *'job for life'* evaporates and we all become what Harold Jarche calls *'artisan workers'* to a greater or lesser extent, individuals who own our skills and are responsible for our own development, the nature of relationship with employers changes [http://www.jarche.com/2013/02/the-new-artisans-of-the-network-era/]. If I can't get what I want here, I'll go elsewhere. You can control the technology, but you can't control the conversation, and when push comes to shove, it's the conversation that counts. Technology is transient and adaptable. I can just bring my own device.

This is just one more example of how historic notions of control exerted by organisations over individuals are failing: technology used to be the preserve of the organisation, because (unless you were one of the geeks) only organisations had the purchasing power and skills to manage it. Now, with cloud based services and every phone smarter than the Apollo lander, mastering technology is not the issue: being productive with it is, and that's where communities count.

Stories let us join together in formal and progressively less formal communities, each supporting us in different ways. We have professional networks and social ones, each buoyed up by the same notion of social capital: our ability to survive and thrive online, our ability to form bonds, to be generous with our time and expertise, our ability to function as a valued member of the community.

Some of these communities are to do with our work, and may indeed be operated and *'owned'* by organisations, but the conversations are our own. What many organisations fail to recognise is that if they close the space down or control it, the conversations that they don't like won't go away. They will just go elsewhere, where they are not part of them. We are so connected that our challenge isn't to find communities to join, it's to find time to service them all adequately.

One central observation of the Social Age is that we are able to maintain larger numbers of loose social ties, over wider geographies, whilst simultaneously building and maintaining an increased number of stronger and deeper ones. In other words, social technology lets us be more social, over wider distances. As our connections increase, we can specialise them and group them, so that we have different communities for different purposes: some technical, some subject matter related, some purely social.

Anyone who just looks for support within the four walls of their organisation is missing a serious trick. In the Social Age our networks can be broad, generalist or niche. I can turn to experts to help me with semantics, with technology questions, or with moral support.

All of them independent, all able to travel with me wherever I go, connected to me through technology, but surprisingly resilient to background noise.

In the Social Age we constantly evolve. I can no longer afford to be static, I have to be an agile learner, able to reinvent myself in response to environmental inputs, in response to the feedback from my communities.

One of the questions from the University community was *"how do I narrate my learning?"*.

Like this... In iterative social spaces: tell your story, get it wrong the first time but be unafraid to try. Then listen to what people say and decide if you agree or not: this is the reality of the Social Age.

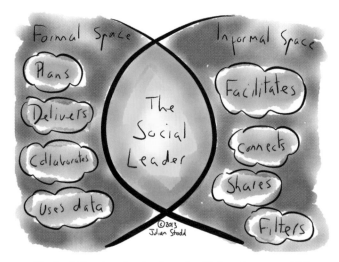

The Social Leader, showing formal and informal space and the
way that the Social Leader sits between the two.

I'm not advocating that we entirely abandon formal learning (or formal leadership), just the opposite, we embrace it, but surround it in progressively less formal layers where we can play with it. Where, in the language of our learning methodology, we can explore and reflect upon it internally. Where I decide how new knowledge stacks up against '*that which I know to be true*' and adapt accordingly, and external reflection, where I share my thinking with the community. It's learning squared, learning cubed, highly iterative, with knowledge as a foundation, but where meaning is co-created within the community.

This is the Social Age: technology has matured enough to facilitate our storytelling and seamlessly enable us to connect and form in meaningful communities. Organisations must adapt too: knowledge is no longer enough. Command and control is outdated, you can lock the doors, but the conversations aren't in the room any more, so it doesn't matter. They're here, in the coffee shop, and around the world.

This reality is the foundation for Social Leadership: the ecosystem is changing. Where meaning is created by communities that exist outside of the formal spaces of the office, we need leadership styles that can do the same. We need to be able to operate in both spaces, highly effectively.

What does this mean?

1. The Social Age is about creating meaning and doing it again, differently, tomorrow

2. Formal and social spaces are colliding: social leaders need to be effective in both

3. The value of knowledge alone is diminishing: it's no longer an effective source of power or sound basis for a business model

4. Communities are 'sense making' entities that we rely on to support our performance

5. Organisations that fail to adapt to the reality of the Social Age will become increasingly less relevant

What should organisations be thinking about this?

1. Explore your organisation's stance towards knowledge: do you hoard it or share it?

2. Explore your relationship with your communities: do you engage or spectate?

3. Ensure your stance towards technology is fluid: the age of the dinosaur systems is over, are you constrained by your technology or liberated by it?

The Social (and socially responsible) Business

The Social Age requires Social Businesses: or to be more precise, *socially responsible* ones.

Being a social business isn't about having a conscience or a great environmental policy: it's about being engaged with the realities of the Social Age: an age when the fundamental relationship between employer, employee and customer is changing. An age when change is constant and our ability to form alliances, build trust and remain agile is key. An age when technology isn't something that sits in a server room and needs air-conditioning: it's something that sits in your pocket and makes you more capable. It's an age when traditional hierarchies of power and authority are crumbling. It's here today and we all live in it. Even if we're not yet ready for it.

The Social Business is prepared to examine the status quo and adapt its processes, methodologies and culture. They engage in conversations with their leaders, their staff, their clients and even their competitors.

A truly Social business will create spaces for experimentation, safe and permissive environments for development. Later, we will explore the nine core skills of Social Leadership, we will look at how they are built over time, through rehearsal. They don't land fully formed.

There needs to be an understanding of risk, not an avoidance of it: avoiding risk can stagnate you. Quantifying it and using it makes you agile.

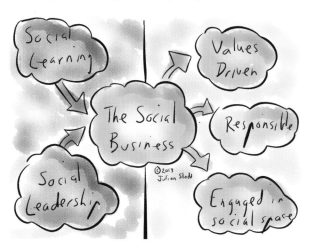

The Social Business benefits from Social Learning approaches and Social Leadership: it's values driven and engaged in all spaces.

Social businesses recognise that they exist in formal spaces, that they own and control, but largely in seml formal and informal spaces, which they don't. Their behaviour and conversations in these seml formal spaces largely defines their future potential and certainly impacts on their magnetism.

Having effective conversations means you have to trust people, empower them to talk on your behalf, because, as far as the customer and community are concerned, the person talking to them on Twitter isthe organisation, hence, Social Leadership bridges the formal and social spaces and has to have authority in both.

This devolution of brand power and identity to individuals and out into the community is a key feature of the Social Age. Organisations still need process, but they don't need scripts: they need relationships with their teams that demonstrate trust and integrity, both things that build over time and form part of the new social contract

In the Social Age, Brand value is substantially created by community.

Synchronicity is important to social businesses: they respond in a timely manner, when times are good or bad, not just when they want to broadcast the news. A social business is proud to be right, but unafraid to say when it gets things wrong. It knows how to find out what the *'buzz'* is, because it has it's ear to the ground, and it builds a reputation for responding honestly and meaningfully. A *'company philosophy'* has no meaning: responding to my Tweet does. Listening to my concerns and responding is more powerful than just acknowledging that I'm annoyed. Social businesses respond in a timely manner, whatever the story.

Technology forms a backbone of social businesses, crossing both formal and informal types, but above all, it's used to facilitate experience, it's used for communication (both internal and external, to facilitate individuals to engage). It's used for collaboration (for formal and informal communities). It's used for facilitation - to deliver scintillating customer journeys, learning journeys, development journeys and employment journeys. It's used to support products and services with active engagement in communities and to respond to challenges. It's used to support excellence and there is a mindset for technology, not just policies.

Social Leaders are not just grown from within, they are attracted from outside. The social business is magnetic to talent: it not only grows it's own Social Leaders and socially engaged teams, but it's viewed as a place to be. It's reputation precedes it, in the labour marketplace as well as the consumer one. Being magnetic to talent isn't about being a Silicon Valley giant: it is about trust and integrity, about equality, about flexibility, support and freedom of expression. It's about living values, not capturing them in a handbook.

Agility in relationships is important too: internally, recognising that careers include raising families and taking holidays, but externally in agile relationships with suppliers, partners and associates. We recognise that, in social businesses, not everyone vital to our success is within these four walls and that not everyone wants to be here forever: it's about sailing on the high seas but knowing who else is around you, and maintaining good relationships with as many as possible. In the Social Age, people come and go, but networks and relationships persist: your ability (and the ability of the organisation to maintain these relationships) is a key differentiator.

And most of all, social businesses can learn (within those experimental spaces they've created): they make mistakes and learn from them, they experiment and learn from it, they listen to their teams, their communities and their customers and they respond. They are bold and they are agile: able to create meaning today and to do it again tomorrow.

The social ecosystem is complex: individuals operating in open communities, engaged with various business in varied ways, supported by social technology and delivering innovative goods and services to a client base that ultimately owns the brand. Building trust with these communities, especially for big businesses like banks that are bruised, is tough.

Organisations need to develop social mindsets: they have to understand the ecosystem and be able to operate at the speed and with the agility required to thrive. They have to cultivate meaningful relationships, social contracts with their employees. Because if they don't, they won't be here tomorrow to feel the benefits.

The Social Age sees a changing nature of work: the office is dead, replaced by agile and mobile working methods, global collaboration and a changing relationship with knowledge. Whilst organisations used to operate in silos, constrained within the granite walls, today the walls are in our heads. The question of the responsibilities of a Social Business is a wide one. where there is no long term continuity of employment, where our development is in our own hands (because businesses focus on reactive and immediate responses to the pressure of change), we need a stronger social contract in place.

Legal and ethical imperatives may vary: but an organisation's responsibility is to curate a strong reputation through thought, act and deed, and the contract with employees forms part of this. This is beyond simply having a sustainability policy and exploring carbon offset: it's about fundamentally how organisations treat employees and how they reap the benefits of operating fairly (as opposed to simply complying with legislation).

We see this clearly around gender equality: it's possible to comply within the law whilst still remaining an unequal employer. We shouldn't need to wait for the legislation to catch up to realise that simple things could be made better. Why can't maternity leave be split between both parents? If we fail to recognise that either mother or father could be the primary caregiver at home, we are complying with the law, but breaching a social responsibility. A responsibility to be fair.

The culture of an organisation is co-created by both individuals and the organisation itself: framed by the company, but lived by the people. The small decisions impact upon it as much as the larger strategic drives. For example, where they pay tax is a strategic decision, but also one that impacts on culture. And indeed, impacts on brand value, because the value of the brand, as we have seen, is owned largely by the social community that surrounds it.

Learning informs brand value: an organisation that supports learning, that values it, will be stronger than one that doesn't. Agility is gained through the ability to create meaning and respond to change, a capability born from mindset as much as technology or strategy.

The Social Business needs to be aware of all these issues: it needs a socially responsible contract with employees, it needs a socially aligned strategy and it needs to listen as much as to talk. But none of this should be seen as fluffy or soft: in the Social Age, I believe that only those businesses that face up to these challenges have a future. The reputation economy is here: how we are perceived matters.

It's good to see many businesses taking up this challenge, but they need support at every level and we all have our part to play. Responsibility is a mindset, not a policy.

What does this mean?

1. The social business recognises that it's responsibilities go beyond complying with what's legal: they need to do what's right

2. They recognise that even though the nature of work is changing, they have a responsibility to develop and support social leaders and workers

3. Reputation counts more than anything

4. Brand is owned by the community, not the marketing team. Actively curate it

What should organisations be thinking about this?

1. Are their processes, mindset and methodologies for business anchored in compliance or responsibility?

2. Is culture fit for purpose?

3. Do they understand the function of the office: is it where meaning is created, or is it an outdated monument to older forms of power and authority, status and reputation, now subverted by more agile modes. And if that's the case, do they have a plan to deal with it?

The social contract

Are you still going to be in that job next year? In five years? Twenty? Chances are that none of us have a job for life, or that we expect to have one. Careers these days are fragmented. They evolve, fracture, make unexpected turns and leaps and take us in surprising directions, only some of which feels under our control.

In older ages, the organisations we worked for owned our careers: from your first graduate position right up to your first promotion, your team leader role, management and, eventually a parking space. Then, one day, they would give you a carriage clock and send you on your way, into retirement. Your useful and productive days behind you.

But no more: today, you'll be made redundant twice before you're thirty five and the chances of getting a parking space are slim. Instead of a large office and membership of the executive lounge, you're more likely to oversee a range of *change* projects and then be part of a transition team as your company merges. Then you'll spend six months in consultation before they say *thanks* and goodbye, leaving you with enough money for a month in India before you start again. And retirement? In the reputation economy, that's a far more fluid affair.

But the Social Age is not about abandoning the values and principles that govern good employment: it's about expanding and enhancing them. The Social Age requires a social contract between employer and employee, based upon fairness, values, integrity and support, but recognising that the very nature of employment has changed.

Organisations used to provide the four walls of an office and a telephone, computer and chair: but what use are these in the Social Age? The office is wherever my iPad sits and the beige walls constrain me far more than they enable me: the Social Age is about creating meaning, about effectiveness and transformation, riding the waves of change, not paddling along behind them. Just as the requirements of work are changing, so to are the things we need to look for in the social contract.

Everyday pressures drive organisations to look for the lowest common denominator: but that has to be countered by the need to be magnetic to talent in a global marketplace. Social Leaders will be developed from within and attracted from outside, but only if there's a fair social contract in place: we have to recognise that magnetism is important and people have choices.

It's not enough to be cost effective and streamlined if you can't attract or retain the very best talent, because that talent is what will make you agile, it's what gives you creativity, and creativity is the magic that will keep your organisation in play five years from now.

Innovation around products, services, structure, cost models and technology: innovation is essential to any healthy organisation, but as the social contract fails, it's harder to find.

A truly social organisation must pay heed to this and go beyond the traditional metrics and bounds of employment: they must do what's right, not what's legislated for. A social business needs to recognise the evolved nature of the marketplace and understand the drivers and pressures on those that inhabit it.

They need to support the development of skills and behaviours that will allow us to thrive in this job, then help us get the next one. If we recognise that there is no longer a job for life, the very least we can do is ensure we attract the best talent, develop it whilst we are aligned, and leave on good terms. In a portfolio labour market, chances are we will work together again down the line anyway.

Things like maternity and paternity leave: don't lag behind, don't take the most defensive position possible. Be bold, brave and do what's right, offering equal terms to both parents.

The Social Contract should recognise that the walls of an organisation are highly permeable: people belong to communities that transcend geography and sector. Our brand, the reputation of the business, resides largely in those spaces. Have a bad reputation and you can't be magnetic to talent, and if you're not magnetic to talent, you're not in a good place at all.

The Social Age presents challenges and opportunities to both employer and employee: as the fundamental mechanics of the workplace evolve, driven by both technology and social pressures, we need to adapt, but not to retreat to the most conservative place and lowest common denominator. We need to be bold, to implement a new social contract that recognises these evolved realities and leaves an organisation able to face these challenges with pride.

What does this mean?

1. As the Social Contract evolves, sticking with older models of recruitment and development will leave you wallowing in the shallows

2. A fair social contract will increasingly make you magnetic to talent: talent which is hard to find and harder to keep, but which is essential for agility

What should organisations be thinking about this?

1. Is your Social Contract balanced?

2. Are you developing enough long term skills within a population, or do you fear that this will just enable people to leave for the next job?

Social Collaborative Technology

The correlation between technology and social leadership is clear: without the technology, you can't be a social leader. You can be a sociable one, but that's a different thing altogether. Social Leadership is grounded within and alongside our communities, those communities that consist of wide and loose social ties combined with a number of strong and deep ones, independent of geography and, increasingly, language.

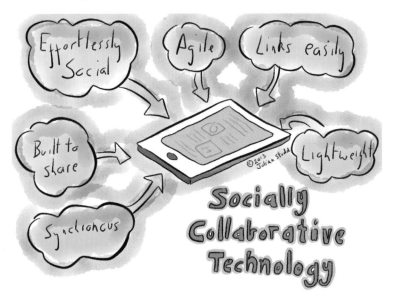

Socially Collaborative Technology is that which connects and facilitates us: this is the most important thing to understand. The technology itself is irrelevant: it's the facilitation that counts.

The clue being in the title, it's effortlessly social. It's everywhere: on our networks, in our pockets, plugged into our ears and our TVs. We can't escape the proliferation of socially collaborative technologies, wherever we try to hide. It draws us into communities around our favourite reality TV show, it permeates our choices of which books to buy and what device to read or listen to them on, it lets us run projects worldwide and, if we are very lucky, it helps us to make sense of the world around us.

The Social Age is founded upon social technology for collaboration and we are just at the start of recognising the potential that it will bring. For Social Leaders, who rely on the amplification and sense making functions of these communities, it's the technology that connects them, that enables them to collaborate.

When I wrote about Mobile Learning, I called the book 'Mindset for mobile learning', because it's not about the technology per se, it's about what we do with it, how we craft more effective and dynamic learning experiences through that technology. Which chipset it contains may facilitate that capability, but it's not the direct cause. It's the same with social collaboration, as many organisations know to their cost: you can invest all you like in systems that have 'social' in the title, but if they're not truly collaborative technologies, they won't build a community and they won't help us to create meaning.

Organisations have to move beyond ownership and into engagement. Don't seek to own the boxes, devices and cables, seek to engage in the conversations.

Truly socially collaborative technology makes it effortless for us to engage, to curate and to share. Like Facebook. It's virtually synchronous, which makes our encounters more conversational, more about storytelling than about publication. True social tech is agile and links easily: it doesn't tie you in with licence agreements, platform specific functionality and endless login and registration pages. Truly social technology is about experience, not IT skills.

The dinosaurs are dead: I believe that the time of those large, legacy systems that cost a fortune to install and never really did what you expected are gone. The future is about smaller, more interconnected technology that fits the social model: it talks to other systems, generates meaningful analytics and lets you act upon them easily. It adapts to context and location.

We were out walking yesterday, a group of friends from University, and the subject came onto books: but instead of which books we were reading, we were talking about the ways we consume the content. Kindles, Kobos and iPads, even audiobooks. There was a constant theme: none of us had the answer. We are all experimenting, finding our way. There is no one system that is going to deliver all the functionality and features that you need to support social learning and social leadership. There may well be one mindset though: a mindset for curation, sharing and collaboration. Mindsets persist whilst technology goes through an endless cycle of development and updates.

Get your mindset right and the rest will fall into place: it's all about collaboration and finding technology that facilitates it.

What does this mean?

1. Technology is at the heart of the Social Age

2. It powers collaboration and is effortlessly social

3. Organisations have limited capability to manage the 'effortless' part of this and, indeed, often cripple the attempt

4. We need a mindset for technology that involves experimentation and agility

What should organisations be thinking about this?

1. Don't try to procure a solution to social collaboration: look for where the conversations are happening and try to engage. On the community's terms.

2. Owning technology, controlling behaviours, is not a win. Collaboration and co-creation is the win. Aim for that

A note on *'agility'* and what it has to do with Social Leadership

Social Leaders make an organisation agile. What is agility?

It's about **QUESTIONING** everything. Just because you did it that way yesterday doesn't mean we should do it that way tomorrow. In the Social Age, change is constant. Doing what you always did won't work anymore. Question everything. It's a good habit for agility.

LEARNING is constant if you're agile. If you're not learning, you're stagnant, lethargic, stuck. Agile learners reach into their networks and communities to create meaning. They use technology to access knowledge and refine it, filter it, share it and tease out the relevance.

REFINING is the process of filtering out the meaningless and contextualising the rest. Agile learners and social leaders do this constantly, curating a reputation for quality.

DOING is better than thinking too hard. Agility is about getting stuck in, but constantly refining. It's an Action Research mindset, about making mistakes and learning.

MISTAKES are inevitable: organisations that want to be agile need to create permissive environments for us to trip up in as we learn.

EDITING is how we refine our actions, how we make the small changes that make us agile.

NARRATING is core to agility: do it, then reflect on it, then share how you did it.

SHARING everything.

In the Social Age, only the agile will thrive.

Approaching Social Leadership: the Ecosystem of the Social Age

Let's draw some of these strands together to understand the ecosystem of the Social Age and how it forms the environment where Social Leadership can thrive.

A map of the Ecosystem of the Social Age: it's a partly uncharted territory, but clearly a new world.

Driven by technology, in a context of wider social change, everything is in flux.

Social technology has facilitated enhanced communication: barriers of time and geography are removed, enabling us to develop and maintain wider communities of loose social ties (as well as deeper, stronger ties with certain people over wider geographies). This drives community formation and function: stronger, wider, deeper. We can view technology as a driving and facilitating force, but it's matched by evolved social skills, particularly driven by social networking. We have learnt through Facebook and it's ilk to live in online communities, developing curatorial and publishing skills to thrive in these spaces.

The most often heard excuses I get from organisations as to why social learning or leadership isn't for them is always along the lines of "*our community don't really get technology*" or "*they never engage*". There's a reason for that: it's because more often than not the technology on offer is redundant, tightly controlled and non permissive for experimentation and the reason people don't engage is because it's not effortless or it doesn't make them more effective. Once organisations realise that they don't need to own everything and have a central city office to be magnetic to talent, to have status, they can start to be more agile, more responsive, more effective.

One of the most fascinating changes technology has brought us is an evolved approach to publishing, with every device of consumption being a device of production. As Clay Shirky taught us, publishing is democratised through multitudinous software solutions. From WordPress to Twitter and Facebook, Yammer and LinkedIn (and a million others) we can share easily. We can produce videos, animation, music, photos, any creative and collaborative venture with ease.

So collaborative technology and democratisation of publishing power change. Publishing directly supports Curation and Reputation, two of the components of the NET model.

Within the ecosystem of the Social Age, we've seen the nature of work change too: away from careers towards portfolios: agility being key. You're unlikely to stay in one place for long, either through choice or redundancy. We've seen how this has led to a revised underlying social contract, as well as different ownership of '*career*' and '*development*'. We now own our own agenda. Organisations and individuals need to adapt to this view: transferable skills and abilities as well as the ever present support we feel from communities.

Remember that brand is no longer owned by marketing teams and flash agencies: it's owned substantially by community: the older model of advertising was one way. Pay enough and you can push your message to everyone. Today, everyone pushes back and has a loud voice to go with it. But it's not all bad news for organisations: as they increasingly want to operate in socially responsible ways, the Social Age brings them the tools and capabilities to do so. Sustainable, agile, fair.

Culture is important in any map of change in the Social Age: I've been exploring how cultures form and respond to change, working on a model of slow degradation followed by fracture. It's about alignment of core values and outward behaviours: what does it cost you to be in a culture?

Finally (at least on this high level map!) is our evolved relationship with knowledge: as we recognise the true impact of the reputation economy and the Social Age, what you know is less important than what you can do with it, your ability to create meaning.

To navigate the Social Age, we need certain skills: Social Leadership, collaboration, curation, storytelling, humility, sharing. It's a long list, but success comes through proper planning. And none of it is rocket science: it's about understanding the environment and ensuring we remain agile as we navigate it.

What does this mean?

1. We are in a new world: everything is changing and much of that change requires new skills to flourish

2. Brand and reputation are increasingly owned by the community

3. As our relationship with knowledge evolves, as the ability to create meaning defines the Social Age, the ground is ripe for Social Leadership

What should organisations be thinking about this?

1. Understand the ecosystem

2. Challenge yourself to challenge process and hierarchy: it may be past it's sell by date

3. Understand who is responsible for this change? Will you be able to co-create and co-own it?

Part 2: The NET Model of Social Leadership

Part 2: The NET Model of Social Leadership

In the first part of this book we explored the foundations of the Social Age. Now it's time to look at the NET Model of Social Leadership in detail. It's called the NET model after the initials of it's three Dimensions (some creative thinking applied here...). *'Narrative'*, *'Engagement'* and *'Technology'*.

Narrative is about *'curation'* (knowledge management and sense-making), *'storytelling'* (communication skills and storytelling culture) and *'sharing'* (adding value and building reputation).

In 'Engagement' we break into the importance of building *'community'*, *'reputation'* (exploring how we use a magnetic model to build it and how it subverts hierarchy in the Social Age) and *'authority'* (how it impacts on communication and how it's fluid in communities).

For *'technology'* we explore *'collaboration'*, looking at social technology and understanding the dynamics of how we co-create meaning, we look at the notion of 'social capital' and how leaders need to help build and share it, and we explore 'co-creation' through facilitating technologies (how we create meaning together and the role of this in asynchronous environments). Technology is also about how this is facilitated and how we ensure nobody is left behind.

Social leaders need to understand and master all three dimensions.

There are common themes: narrative runs through everything, through three levels. There is *'personal narrative'*, our individual learning, there's the *'co-created narrative'*, forged in social spaces and communities, and there's *'organisational narrative'*, the story of change that the organisation narrates. The three are interlinked.

Reputation and authority are also deeply embedded throughout: reputation is founded upon curatorial skills, forged in communities and facilitated by technology.

For each component I'm also showing an outer layer, with some specific tools and concepts that can be explored further. This layer is likely to continue developing: as Harold Jarche says, we're in constant beta. Specifically, I'm developing some online diagnostic tools to look at capability in some areas.

What we end up with then is a journey from the centre circle, which is a conceptual view defining the three Dimensions, through to the nine components, which define specific skills, and then out to the actual diagnostics and tools to use in the workplace.

To master a social model of Leadership, a model suitable for the Social Age, we need first to understand the context, the evolving nature of work and the roles of community, then we need to master specific technical and social skills to be successful. This book will cover both these elements, exploring the realities of work and life in the Social Age and a practical model for developing leaders.

The 1st Dimension of Social Leadership: Narrative in the NET Model

Narrative is about understanding how we communicate in stories, about how we can shape and influence these to be effective leaders in the Social Age. It covers the way we find things out, the ways we interpret them, the ways we share that information in stories and how we interact with other people whilst we do so.

We communicate in stories: building personal, group and organisational stories and '*narrative*' crosses all three of these boundaries. As a Social Leader, we need to understand how we narrate our personal story, how we develop that in teams into a co-created narrative and how that relates to and shapes the overall organisational narrative. Narratives are fluid, evolving over time and in response to circumstances, but they are not out of our control: we have the ability to shape and influence them.

Curation focuses on three states: '*discovery*', '*perception*' and '*interpretation*'. Discovery is about how we find things out, Perception's about seeing the structure and Interpretation is about finding the meaning, contextualising it to our reality. Curation is an active skill, not a passive one: it's about identifying gaps in skills and knowledge and plugging them, but also about building communities and networks. Curation is a continuous process, forming a foundation for the stories we tell.

> *Practical: the practical activities that will relate to curation are around knowledge management methodologies, around filtering and around unconscious bias.*

Within the Storytelling component of Social Leadership, we are looking at how stories work, about shape, structure, tone of voice and interconnection (how they relate to other stories). We need to understand the theory of storytelling, exploring how stories contain information and how that information is structured and perceived, in order to develop coherent narratives, stories that make sense in isolation and when connected to our individual realities.

> *Practical: the practical activities that will relate to storytelling include practicing different stances, exploring how stories convey meaning and crafting messages from multiple viewpoints.*

Sharing is about inward and outward facing realities and reciprocity. Later we will cover the social technologies that facilitate sharing, but for now we are interested in how relationships are reinforced through sharing, the differences between synchronous and asynchronous sharing and how sharing is a differentiating skill in the Social Age.

Practical: activities to develop sharing skills would include mapping a communication strategy, looking at perspectives and scheduling.

Narrative is the first dimension of Social Leadership: it's about how we curate our knowledge and skills, how we understand our boundaries and limitations and how we tell meaningful, engaging stories to effect change. Narrative forms a foundation for engagement and is facilitated by technology.

The 2nd Dimension of Social Leadership: Engagement in the NET Model

The realities of leadership are changing: positional authority is being subverted by reputation, built in communities. For this reason, Social Leaders have to be more agile, more able to respond to the synchronous dialogues of the social era, able to connect in communities and reciprocate effectively. Social Leadership is very much about actions in the moment, within a mindset that develops reputation over time.

Community is the reality of the Social Age: we come together in communities to learn, to explore, to challenge and to co-create shared meaning. Communities may be emergent and short lived, formed around specific challenges or projects, or they may be personal learning networks that travel with us throughout our careers. Communities may be entirely social or completely formal: they are often specialist and we belong to and contribute within a wide range.

Not all communities are the same: learning communities tend towards more structure, a scaffolded approach to discussion, whilst fully social ones are less structured, happy to move with the trends. Social Leaders need to be able to engage within communities with humility and consistency: they need to develop a tone of voice that helps build reputation, but reputation will be formed on quality of curation and storytelling, skills we explored under '*Narrative*'.

Social Leadership skills around community are about participation and creation: sometimes taking part in active communities, but as leaders they also need to be able to form spontaneously emergent ones around specific challenges, drawing upon their reputation to build and sustain these. Social Capital is a key concept, and developing this in others a key skill.

> *Practical: exercises around mapping communities and our participation within them, developing social capital in others and around tone of voice for engagement. Moderation skills and an understanding of the lifecycle of moderation are also valuable.*

In the Social Age, reputation is vital and it's under our control: reputation is founded upon our actions, our responses, our tone of voice and stance. It's built, forged, in real time within our communities and a strong reputation is the hallmark of a good leader. Reputation in the Social Age is based upon our ability to create meaning and to help others to do the same: it's usually less about knowledge, more about agility, the skills to find things out and synthesise those things into an interpretation, creating new meaning. Then taking action: reputation is about getting things done and supporting others as they do the same.

In the Social Age, humility and sharing are key reinforcers to reputation, recognising the agile nature of work and roles within teams. Indeed, I've often said that Social Leadership is a fluid role, defined by the moment, not by a job title: good Social Leaders will sometimes pass the baton round when circumstances warrant it. It's contextual and consensual.

> *Practical: exercises around narration, stance, authenticity and tone of voice help us to think about reputation. Developing skills to understand the role of reciprocity.*

The nature of Authority is changing: away from positional, hierarchical authority, more about reputation driven impact. Newer models are subverting the old. The Social Leader needs to recognise the source of their authority (through developing reputation) and be effective at using that power (through honing narrative and community skills).

The foundations of authority in the Social Age are within community, it's this grassroots connection that allows social leaders to be truly agile, to deploy their networks in support of change, indeed, to welcome change (because they recognise that change is constant and presents opportunities).

> *Practical: models of authority and recognising our style, self diagnostics to map areas of influence, developing agility in forms of response, influence and contracting with teams.*

The Engagement dimension of Social Leadership is all about connecting with communities and teams and delivering change. Reputation gives us authority, grounded within community. Engagement is where things happen. It's the thing most desired by organisations and the thing that can only be built on integrity and humility in the Social Age.

The 3rd Dimension of Social Leadership: Technology

Technology isn't about software and code, but rather about how technology facilitates community building, delivers experiences. We're looking at how Social Leaders need to use technology to foster and support Narrative and Engagement, looking at how the first two dimensions rely on the third.

Social Leadership is inherently collaborative: it's about communities. Social Leaders need to recognise the function of communities and support both their establishment (in agile ways around challenges and projects) as well as understanding their role and the processes of moderation and support. The role of technology in communities is largely around facilitation and dissemination: our PCs, smartphones and iPads provide access whilst we are on the move, meaning a shift towards more synchronous engagement in dialogue. '*Little and often*' is the order of the day: collaborative learning spaces are not deeply reflective, but they are partially so.

The value is more in the dialogue and the sharing than thinking of it like your life's work (there are exceptions, but broadly Isee these collaborative community spaces as conversations with an extra dimension added). There is more room to think than in a straight conversation, but the meaning is still emergent from the group, it's not the highly reflective space of a book or article. They rely on a pace of dialogue, on the speed and responsiveness of conversation.

Collaboration is about forming mutually beneficial relationships, but the benefits may not be synchronous: you build credit against your reputation that may be cashed in later. Collaboration takes place within communities, but the existence of a community does not guarantee collaboration: it needs to be fostered. When this is done using technology, it differs from '*in the real world*', and that's why '*community*' falls under Engagement, but 'collaboration' sits within technology. We have to understand the tools at our disposal.

Within Technology, we need to explore methods for understanding and mapping collaboration, strategies for collaboration and how people engage and form relationships. It's about understanding reciprocity. Understanding these foundations lets us more effectively structure our interventions and inputs, helping us derive maximum value.

Collaboration falls under '*Technology*' because I'm particularly interested in how we use technology to remain engaged with those groups whilst we are on the move, whilst we are within our everyday reality rather than the abstract classroom or workshop.

Practical: community mapping exercises and ways of characterising modes of interaction within those spaces, as well as strategies for engagement in an agile way. Methods for assessing which spaces to use to support new communities and how technology can facilitate our leadership style.

Social Capital is one's ability to survive and thrive in collaborative online communities: it's about success in engagement, about safeguarding people against mistakes and about preventing anyone being disenfranchised through skill or technology. It's part of the role of the Social Leader to have high social capital, but also to utilise a range of methodologies to develop this in others.

Trust and integrity are important concepts in the development of social capital: relationships are based on these but, in the Social Age, where personality is projected into virtual spaces, things are not as clear as you might think. Social spaces are not independent of context: what will my employer think, what will my friends and colleagues think, what are the consequences of conversations? Social Leaders have to have the skills to ensure nobody is left behind, to ensure that collaboration is fostered through great conversations and narratives, not controlled through policies and punishment. Collaboration relies on clarity and fairness.

Practical: we have to explore methodologies for building social capital (as well as identifying exclusion and addressing it). Recognising disenfranchisement and strategies for engagement. Identifying what's 'fair' and incorporating that into our decision making.

The co-creation of meaning is one of my favourite topics: it's about how we come together to learn and it ties in with other areas I've explored previously around music and narrative. When we learn, we create meaning out of knowledge, out of what we find out. Meaning is personal, contextual, time limited and evolving: it's created in the moment and moves over time.

Within groups, we go through a process of co-creation, where consensus is reached and methodologies applied to deal with dissent. In the Social Age, this conversation takes place in real spaces as well as online communities and within our networks, through synchronous and asynchronous conversations. Understanding the process, being able to facilitate and participate in the co-creation of meaning is a key social leadership skill.

It's about understanding how people come together to make sense of the world around them, how we cope with and thrive on change, how relationships are formed and evolve and how we respond to new inputs as a group. It's the living, breathing heart of how organisations work: creating meaning as a group. This is what shapes organisational culture and thinking.

As with collaboration, our '*technology*' focus here is on understanding the realities of how this works in the Social Age, facilitated by technology, but all about people.

> *Practical: exercises in co-creation, understanding roles within communities (subject matter, information, validator, narrator etc), flexibility in role and stance in community, negotiating responsibly.*

The 9 skills of Social Leadership

Now that we've seen an outline of the Three Dimensions, it's time to delve into the detail of the nine core skills that sit underneath them.

1st Dimension:
Narrative Skill 1: Curation in Social Leadership

The 1st Dimension in the NET Model of Social Leadership is Narrative. Curation is one part of this, and it's to do with how we shape our presence, how we curate our reputation and our selves in the world around us.

"Curation focuses on three states: discovery, perception and interpretation. Discovery is about how we find things out, Perception is about seeing the structure and Interpretation, finding the meaning, contextualising it to our reality. Curation is an active skill, not a passive one: it's about identifying gaps in skills and knowledge and plugging them, but also about building communities and networks. Curation is a continuous process, forming a foundation for the stories we tell."

We can view *'curation'* as taking control of something we do naturally: we all curate our presence, whether we think about it or not. What shoes you wear, how your hair is cut, what car you drive, who you send Birthday cards to: these are all curatorial acts. As we define our personas, create the spaces that we live and work in, then we also fill in the gaps: we learn new skills, buy new clothes, make new contacts to expand and shape our lives in specific ways.

In a museum, the curator has many responsibilities: they find and bring new artefacts into the collection, with an eye on the value of that object in isolation, but also in the context of the rest of the collection. An original Apple Macintosh computer may be nice in isolation, but in the context of a display showing the complete sequence of development through to the iPad today, it's got greater value. Context is everything.

But it's not enough to just have something within the collection: we have to be able to identify and articulate the value. We have to be able to interpret it within a context for the recipient (which I'll cover in more detail around *'interpretation'* in due course...)

In the NET Model, we explore three facets of Curation: *'Discovery'*, *'Perception'* and *'Interpretation'*. This is really about how we find things out, how we make sense of them and how we share them, adding context.

'Discovery' is about placing a stake in the ground and identifying what actions you will take to support that space: what space will you claim as a leader? Do you specialise in particular areas, such as technical project management, legal or operations, or are you a generalist? Do you specialise around projects or around developing teams? In the Social Age, agility is key, but we will also each curate areas of specialism. You need to lay some foundations for reputation as a Social Leader, and once you have done this, you can start to fill in the gaps.

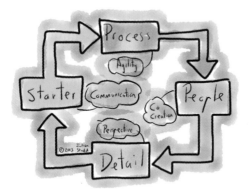

I'm toying with this format as a structure for this diagnostic exercise: It's a reflective exercise to think about where you add the most value. Are you all about ideas? Are you a starter? Are you about the detail, do you put the structure in place? Are you about people, forming and deploying teams, inspiring and supporting, or are you about process and compliance, controlling costs and timescales? You probably do a bit of all of these, but where do you see your strengths? They are all aspects of agility.

If you are a **Starter**, you need to discover how to be a superb communicator. If you are all about the **Detail**, you need to understand perspective. If you are for **People**, then facilitating co-creation is key and in **Process**, it's about agility in the Social Age. As an exercise, individuals would work to determine their perceived strengths, then think about how to discover communities and skills to reinforce these.

What this means:

1.　What we share impacts on how people perceive us: we have control over this

2.　It's not just what you share, but how you contextualise it that counts

3.　Quality trumps quantity: make it relevant and it's more likely to be amplified

How to develop these skills:

1.　Rehearsal: you need to find your authentic tone of voice

2.　Learn your strengths: are they aligned with how other people see you?

3.　Cultivate strong networks that specialise in specific areas: you are not alone, you need community to curate effectively

1st Dimension:
Narrative Skill 2: Storytelling in Social Leadership

Social Leadership is about ethical decision making and acting with integrity and transparency to deliver the promises of a new social contract, where employer and employee both need to find value.

Storytelling is a nuanced activity: it's worth deconstructing it to explore the components.

We communicate in stories: establishing commonality and sharing values. From the earliest stories warning us against wandering off alone at night or why we need to be wary of strangers, through to tales of nation building and love, stories are the units in which we create and share meaning.

Cultures build their histories around stories, but stories are not truth: they are an interpretation, flavoured and coloured by our preconceptions, our history, viewpoint and context. Stories are intensely personal but highly subjective.

Within social leadership, I use three components for Narrative: 'Curation', 'Storytelling' and 'Sharing'. Curation, as we've seen, is about determining the content for your stores, it's about curating the space that you will be known for and determining what will add value as opposed to cluttering up the airwaves. Storytelling involves us determining how to create meaning around the content.

Stories require some structure: we need to consider our stance, our character's, our tone of voice and overall story length, as well as the genre we use and where the bookmarks go.

No learning happens in isolation, so the context for storytelling within an organisation is important: where is your story coming from, is it 'official' or 'informal', am I expected to act upon it or just enjoy it? As Social Leaders, we need to be able to actively choose the styles of our stories and illustrate them accordingly. Formal stories need a particular structure, whilst informal ones may vary. Our stance is the viewpoint from which we start: are we 'alongside' the learner, or are we standing in front of them and explaining things. Are we being directive and telling them that 'this is what the story is', or are we co-creating the meaning alongside them?

We fill our lives with books, but don't use all of them all the time: when choosing to read with my favourite nephew, I choose a particular storybook (a Thomas the Tank Engine one of course), whilst for my niece it's different (frustratingly reinforcing gender stereotypes by being largely pink and involving fairies and ballet). The genre, characterisation, style and length all impact on likely engagement.

Of course, we are not writing novels for our teams, but the principles of what make stories stick are the same: well crafted, coherent, emotionally engaging, free from spelling mistakes!

We also need a good balance of the factual and the social, a balance between just pushing out information (which may not be best done through stories) and pure social chatter (which lacks focus). We need to engage but also inform.

Narrative and story: the words can change, but the narrative remains the same.

It's worth thinking about two elements: *'narrative'* and *'story'*. The narrative is the core informational structure, the story is the words we put around it. Organisations often focus effort on controlling the story, when the narrative is more important. The words can change with each retelling, but the narrative remains the same. It's like the story of the fall of Troy: you can read the original texts, you can read an academic study or a children's book, or you can watch Brad Pitt in the film, but whatever version of the story you experience, the core narrative is the same. It's just retellings of that narrative.

Whilst this is a slightly simplistic view, what I want to emphasise is that you don't have to exert effort trying to control the retellings, you just need to work on the strength and coherence of the core narrative.

Social leaders propagate the seeds of stories within their communities: they set them free to be told and retold, each retelling grounded in the core narrative but taking on it's own story form. Indeed, the process of curation (with it's interpretation and 'sense making') is largely about the reframing of stories to be appropriate and to resonate with our core audiences.

So here is the foundation of a model for shaping and releasing stories as a true Social Leader!

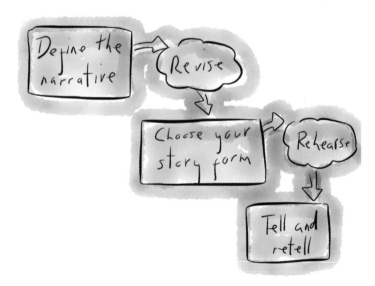

We define a narrative, choose the story form, then tell and retell the story.

It's iterative: first, define the core narrative, but don't set it in stone. With each retelling, as well as the passage of time, we revise and strengthen this (through various social and formal spaces). We need to choose the story form and rehearse our telling of it. The process of telling and retelling it is where we refine our messages and our delivery.

What this means:

1. Storytelling skills are important: but you need to understand the difference between 'story' and 'narrative'

2. Stance, tone of voice and authenticity all impact on how stories are received

3. Strong stories may be amplified: weak stories will fall by the wayside

How to develop these skills

1. Take time to reflect on your narrative and...

2. ...use reflective spaces to refine it

3. Practice the telling and retelling of core stories to develop your stance and vocabulary

1st Dimension:
Narrative Skill 3: Sharing in Social Leadership

I lent Sam my copy of *Business Model Generation* last week. It's a great book, really useful in getting your thoughts straight in the early stages of planning, so I wanted to share it with him as he is working on business strategy right now.

Cath showed me a video on YouTube last night: *Caravan of Thieves*, a band she saw in America when she was playing at a festival there. She thought I'd like to see them next year as I'm planning some US work and may be able to coincide the two.

There's a common theme: both Cath and I saw something, thought it was good, and **shared** it with specific people accordingly, based on our knowledge of their likes, needs and interests. We both put a context around what we shared. We both used an appropriate channel to share it in, and it was timely. When we chose what to share, we were aware that our reputation was at stake: share a long and tedious book, or a song that I hate, and my view of your taste suffers.

Setting appropriate '*Context*', choosing the right '*Channel*' and making our shares '*Timely*' are three skills within Sharing.

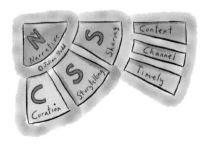

What are we going to share? In the Social Age, the question is more '*what are we going to hide?*'. We share ideas, articles, books, music, we share our time, our feedback, encouragement and support. We Share things that make us laugh or make us better. We find the meaning in things and situations and share that too. Sharing is a key skill of Social Leaders because it contributes to reputation, and reputation drives authority. Reputation is what makes us ultimately effective.

Finding Context is about identifying where the meaning sits for someone else. What's relevant to me today may be of no interest to you in your current context (but may be highly relevant tomorrow, in your next). To define Context, we have to know people: not just their LinkedIn profile and homepage on a corporate intranet, but know them through interaction, through listening and experiencing their reality. Sharing may sound altruistic, but it draws us closer together.

Our Contexts are defined by our everyday reality, by the pressures that surround us and the reward mechanisms that pay us, but also by our history and stance: our ethical perspectives and social values. You can't set a Context effectively without empathy and understanding.

Old school advertising approaches that work on target audiences are outdated here: we are sharing to individuals, to create personal meaning, not mass audiences. Reputation is built incrementally through this, permeating through the nodes and amplifiers within networks, like the President kissing babies as he heads through the Mid West states.

Choosing the Channel to share through is an important decision, impacted by considerations of time, convenience, cost, impact and shared value. Some channels have imbued value: books carry gravitas, LinkedIn is related to businesses and job search, Facebook is more social. These vary by individual (another reason to understand someone's everyday reality). There's no point in me trying to share something with Benoit through Dropbox, because within his corporate reality, it's impossible to access.

Different channels also have different impact: giving someone a book is a tactile as well as emotionally engaging experience. But if we are talking to busy people, if our team is under pressure, a book may not be very useful: perhaps a link to an article (or even a book review) is more relevant. There's also something to consider about what we are sharing and how suitable each channel is for the format and subject matter: reading text on mobiles is tedious, watching videos takes bandwidth, performance support materials should be concise and clear, easy to digest in seconds, not hours.

And don't forget the time: shares can be time critical for different reasons. Sometimes the knowledge expires: telling someone about an event or meeting for example. Sometimes knowledge or shares decay over time: an article may date over a year or two, especially if it relates to technology! Sometimes the timeliness relates to the individual we are sharing with: they may be searching for a new job or facing a specific challenge. Indeed, perceptive Social Leaders will aim to share relevant material within an appropriate context to support people at exactly these times.

Sharing may be about sharing out time: this is where we are sharing our thoughts or ideas and, again, the timing of this may be valuable for us (as we refine and iterate our ideas through our communities, much as I'm doing right now in this draft) and for whoever we share with (where we may trigger thoughts for them too). Sharing is very much a co-creative experience.

What this means:

1. Sharing bolsters reputation: it's about quality, context, relevance and timeliness. Not volume

2. Sharing must be in line with your curated space: if you catch me sharing stories about football, it's incongruous

3. Where you share is as important as what you share: are you up to date with the ecosystem of the Social Age?

How to develop these skills:

1. Explore the channels you can share in: see what other people do and form your sharing plan

2. Consciously consider context and timeliness

3. Take time to get to know people better: use that knowledge to share wisely

2nd Dimension:
Engagement Skill 4: Community in Social Leadership

The Social Age is about communities: communities that are no longer defined by purely physical or geographical borders. Today, our communities crisscross the world, our membership and conversations facilitated by social collaborative technology and shared through the amplification of ideas. Social Leaders need to understand where these communities exist, how to engage in them and how to utilise them to lead effectively.

Unlike in more traditional leadership models, leadership in the communities of the Social Age is through authority based on reputation, not hierarchy. In other words, leadership is earned not bestowed. The power is consensual.

We start by looking at Location. How many communities are visible, how many hidden? A community may be formal and internal, for example, a group of colleagues conversing on a Yammer or Intranet forum, or it may be formal and external, like a professional discussion on LinkedIn. Membership may be entirely drawn from an employed population (typical for an intranet), a combination of employed and contractors, or almost entirely external, beyond traditional organisational control or view. Communities based around professional challenges may fall into this category, such as a community of global project managers or people who are interested in research on Unconscious Bias.

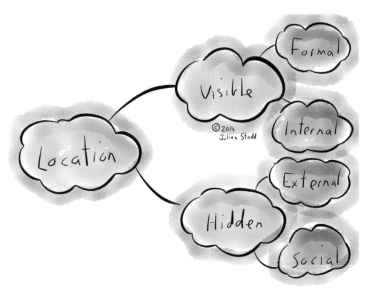

Different communities have different types of conversations and, as a rule, the further away they get from the formal space, the less under the influence of the organisation they are. It's not that organisations can't engage in these conversations: it's just that they have to recognise the seml formal nature of the environment. In the Social Age, the meaning and conversations are co-owned and co-created by communities, not owned and imposed by organisations. That's why Social Leaders have to understand the ecosystem and engage in or phrase conversations accordingly.

Communities serve different purposes: Social Leaders need to understand the different purposes of different communities and adopt an appropriate stance and style as a result. Communities are used for sense making, for creating 'meaning' in Social Age terms, but they are not always about sharing ideas we already understand. They may be about enlightenment: bringing new knowledge and ideas to the members. Within a community, different people will be enlightened in different areas and Social Leaders need to understand where they curate their position and act accordingly.

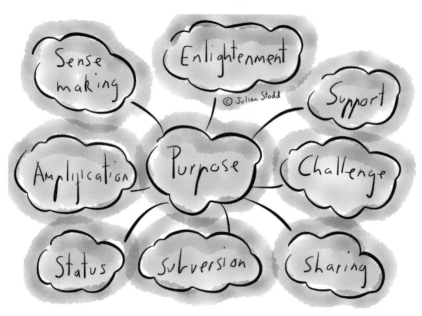

Communities are used for support and challenge: flip sides of the same coin. When we bring ideas or problems to a community to resolve, we can expect both support and challenge. It's this very process that gives community sense-making such value.

Communities can also be used to subvert existing wisdom: this *subversive* nature of communities is important for agile businesses, because they rely on the subversive process to be creative, to be innovative. Existing processes give existing results: sometimes we have to break things to reiterate them in a better frame. But leaders engage in these subversive spaces carefully: the mantle of leadership counts for nothing in subversive spaces and may indeed be a hindrance.

Some communities give us status: professional bodies or exclusive clubs for supporting change. Again, Social Leaders need to understand their terms of engagement in these spaces and may indeed want to create these spaces themselves. Building your own exclusive community for subversives or change agents may be a powerful way of mobilising the seml formal channels in support of your individual and organisational goals. I've been working alongside some Healthcare Radicals groups within the NHS who are doing exactly this: they are subversive, but fully supported by leadership.

Finally, communities can be powerful amplifiers, and amplification is a core feature of the Social Age: understanding how ideas stories are amplified enables us to be heard more widely without shouting more loudly. It's about creating and sharing magnetic stories: sharing wisely.

So what's your role within these communities?

Within our communities, we take many different roles: they are contextual and fluid over time.

We can identify nine functions of the role: to '*Nurture*' individuals and ideas, to '*Support*' the community, to '*Lead*' it in certain areas, to '*Engage*' in other conversations, to '*Crossover*' between communities and share wisdom, to '*Narrate*' the stories that are told, sometimes to '*Moderate*' conversations, to '*Grow*' the community, to '*Facilitate*' change.

With limited time and resources (not to mention emotional energy), Social Leaders need to plan how they engage. We don't want to get stuck in one segment: too much time moderating may be at the cost of nurturing. Too much growth is no good if we aren't getting value by sharing great stories (although conversely, great stories will generate growth, or they will if we share them widely with amplifiers... it's a great circular process!).

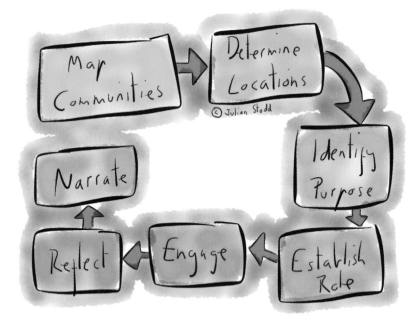

So let's join it together to look at how Social Leaders should approach Community: they need to map the communities to understand the ecosystem of engagement. Once they've determined where the communities are (both the formal and social ones) they can decide on the purpose of each, which will impact whether and how you engage and what role you take (recognising the need to be agile in role over time. Once we're engaged in communities, we pause to reflect on what we gain through membership and, in time, narrate those stories back out into our communities. That's a truly social way of working.

'Community' is the fourth of the Nine skills of Social Leadership. We've looked at it in terms of 'location', 'purpose' and 'role' to establish rules for how and why we engage and what we can expect to get out of it.

What does this mean

1. Communities are the source of reputation and hence authority in the Social Age

2. They are 'sense making' entities, but we have to learn how to engage effectively

3. The purposes that communities serve and our roles within them are fluid: we should seek to understand this to be effective

How to develop these skills:

1. Map your communities and reflect on the purpose each serves: do you have access to the right expertise?

2. Consider your role: are you fluid in your stance and approach. Do you have the right skills when you need to listen?

3. Consciously and constantly review your communities and your approach to working with them: that's agility

2nd Dimension:
Engagement Skill 5: Reputation in Social Leadership

We've covered foundations, but now it's the hard stuff: 'Reputation' and 'Authority'. One gives the other, but in the Social Age, traditional foundations of authority are subverted by more social and fluid forms.

Reputation is not a matter of marketing: it's a matter of actions and intentions. More specifically, the actions that are born of intentions. You can be full of good intentions, but if your actions don't match or exceed them then you're not a Social Leaders. You're probably falling back on more traditional forms of power.

Power: where does it come from?

There are different forms of power, sources of authority. Positional power is the most obvious form of authority: power based in hierarchy and structure. It's the type of power that we codify in institutions and systems and it's the least fluid of them all. There is often a view that hierarchical power is necessary in certain situations, when things need to be decided fast or where clear allocation of risk and responsibility is needed, but this is outdated.

Communities are great sense making spaces, but they don't divest us of individual responsibility. Social approaches don't require us to abandon formal hierarchies, but they do require us to recognise that our hierarchical power may be matched by socially derived forms, based around reputation.

Subject matter expertise is another form of power: simply knowing more than someone else about something (be it nuclear fusion or how to operate the office photocopier). We all derive some of our power through subject matter expertise, it sits within normal social dynamics and powers our stories and conversations. But only the lethargic will rely on their expertise as a foundation for their power in the Social Age, when meaning is what counts, the ability to create meaning based on knowledge. We can easily be left behind if we anchor our reputation to knowledge in the growing storm.

As our relationship with knowledge evolves, so to does how pure knowledge informs reputation and authority.

We see this in healthcare right now: we used to go to the doctor to find out what was wrong with us and to make us better. Today, increasingly, people are accessing pure knowledge online and through communities and turning up to see their doctor with an initial self diagnosis and even expectation of treatment. This doesn't make the role of the doctor redundant: far from it, it changes it from one of pure source of knowledge to practitioner based on ability to join the dots, to work with broad knowledge and experience. Experience is more than knowledge: it's the benefit of multiple stories, the ability to effect change, to impact through action.

Longevity is a source of power: someone who had done something for a long time or who has been in role forever. This is risky though: where the Social Age rewards agility, there is a risk that longevity alone simply means that you are becalmed by familiarity. That wouldn't be an issue if the world was static, but in fact it's changing around our ears and solutions or approaches that worked a year ago may not work now. Agility is the ability to create meaning in the moment and to respond to the change.

We need to reflect on sources of power to see how they are changing as a function of wider changes in society (facilitated by technology).

Reputation is a measure of our standing, a measure of how the community values our input: the greater your reputation, the more you can influence on a particular subject, but also the more willing the community is to tolerate your mistakes. This notion around mistakes is important, especially as formal systems are often somewhat intolerant of failure. If social systems are more willing to provide space to learn, they will inherently continue to grow stronger.

When looking at reputation, we can consider three stages that allow us to take a more active control: '*Navigate*', '*Respond*', '*Evaluate*'.

It's part of actively curating our reputation: to chart a course through all possible actions, recognise when we are responding through habit and reflect on that to see what source of power we are drawing upon, respond to the triggers to moderate our response and then evaluate the effectiveness of that response and quantify how it enhances reputation. Finally we reflect and narrate, staples of '*working out loud*', a reflective approach to developing capability.

Let's look at these in more detail.

Navigation is a mindset: out of all possible courses of action, which one will we take and are we being pushed there by the current or actively choosing the route?

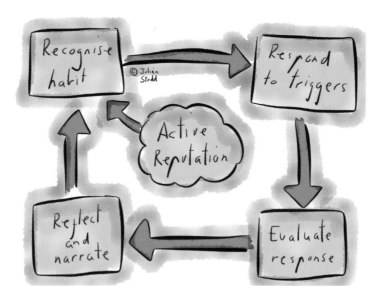

We are creatures of habit, which makes us both effective (because we efficiently deal with recurring situations with the minimum of thinking required) but also lethargic (because we often fail to evolve our responses and to act with agility, testing out new problem solving methods). Habits are neurologically efficient, and effective, but we need to reflect on their appropriateness. Indeed, just *recognising* when we are responding through habit and when through conscious decision making is valuable.

Once we understand our reliance on habit, we can determine our '*triggered responses*': the reason this is important is because triggered responses reinforce reputation, so if we never reflect upon and adapt our responses, we will forever be caught within current reputation.

Because the Social Age is about creating meaning within the moment, it's about action review cycles, testing new approaches and being unafraid to modify them. It's about agility.

'*Evaluating responses*' ensures that we are taking a learning approach, not just firing solutions out into the world and hoping for the best. Responses within communities are far easier to evaluate, because the community provides a narrative, it gives us real time feedback.

Evaluation ties in with notions of amplification: as we learn what works, what reinforces our reputation and makes our stories more effective, we should do more of it.

Finally we '*reflect and narrate*': this being a staple of the Social Age. Reflection is about measuring impact and gauging our learning, it's about inward reflection (how have I changed?) and outward reflection (sharing the story of your learning). We then narrate our learning to the community, to share both the good and the bad, the things we got right and the parts we got wrong. This narrative is an open and honest approach to leadership and directly contributes to our reputation.

Social Leaders need a strong reputation in both formal and social spaces. They need to be adept at '*playing the game*' within the formal spaces (having data driven conversations, influencing, building formal authority), but also at social approaches (challenging and supporting, even subverting inefficient processes and controls). They have to play both games.

We see this with the emergence of the socially active leaders: the blogging and tweeting CEO who is #WorkingOutLoud and directly visible to the community (contrast that to the hierarchical CEO who hides in an ivory tower and rarely meets employees or customers directly on his or her journey from BMW to the lift to the top floor).

Reputation subverts other forms of authority but may, if built well, compliment them. We can have the best of both worlds if we are able to understand what each can give us and be true to both.

What does this mean:

1. Reputation subverts older forms of power, such as positional or hierarchical ones

2. It's forged in social spaces, through actions, not intentions

3. We need to reflect on our responses: are they through habit or by design

How to develop these skills:

1. Learn to recognise habit and the impact it has on reputation

2. Develop active reputation management strategies

3. Learn to effectively narrate your learning which will build your reputation

2nd Dimension:
Engagement Skill 6: Authority in Social Leadership

We could view Authority as the goal of Social Leadership. Or, rather, we could if we remained anchored in 20th century notions of leadership. Authority is not the goal, but it is a means to an end. If we have authority, we are better able to engage in certain communities, our messages carry more weight and are more likely to be amplified (if we curate our space well and tell magnetic stories). Authority in the Social Age is founded upon reputation, forged within our communities.

I need to provide some context here: Social Leadership is not intended to replace other forms, it's complimentary. It just carries Leadership over, out of purely formal ones and into the seml formal spaces that surround it. If we rely on formal, hierarchical forms of power and authority, we limit our influence to formal organisational spaces. At a time when meaning is created in communities, seml formal, crossing boundaries and geographies, forms of power rooted in the formal have limited appeal and leverage.

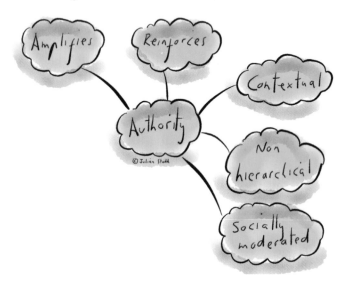

Social Leadership requires engagement: based on trust and integrity. Once we move away from purely formal spaces, boundaries can become unclear, we are creating permissive environments for conversation without always clarifying what types of conversations we will permit. This ambiguity introduces risk for everyone (risks that we may not even realise we have adopted). For example: we create a social collaborative forum and ask people to share ideas for how we can improve the reputation of the business. Someone shares a story about a project they worked on that went wrong and what they learnt from it. At their annual performance review, someone produces this data as evidence of their failed project. Is that fair?

Any notion of authority in Social Leadership needs to take into account these constraints and considerations: the territory can be unclear. Good Social Leaders navigate it, but also help others to do so.

Amplification is a building block of authority, but it relies on this trust being in place: the integrity of any community is founded upon it. Without trust, we cannot effectively engage in a relationship space (although we may engage at a transactional level). Transactional engagement is simply going through the motions: doing what we think is required of us.

This, incidentally, is probably how much organisational training happens. Going through the motions without authenticity, because the risk of opening up is too great.

Authority is based upon our reputation, which is earned from actions, which is why social leadership is about what you do as much as what you say. The stories you tell and the stories that are told about you.

Because the authority of sSocial Leadership is earned, it helps us to amplify our messages, to gain greater traction, which is stronger than the brute force approach that underlies formal hierarchies.

Strong, socially mediated authority reinforces our ability to be effective, in Social Age terms, it reinforces our ability to create meaning within and alongside our communities. This 'sense making' function of communities is highly valuable: co-creative and co-owned, built from the cognitive surplus and investment of many people.

One of the areas of Social Leadership that can be most challenging is it's contextual quality. Whilst within one community I may have authority, in another, I have none. Or, indeed, at a different time within the same community my authority may vary: not because my reputation is damaged, but simply because communities serve different purposes at different times, so leadership (and indeed all the other roles) can be contextual. This is one reason why humility is a desirable trait in Social Leaders: they are willing to put down the mantle of leadership (or indeed have it removed from them for a while) for the wellbeing of the wider community. This is why I describe Social Leadership as 'socially moderated', it always requires permission and framing by the community itself. Anytime we exercise the tools of authority without the permission of community, we are simply falling back on positional authority.

As a side note, it is perfectly possible to have positional authority within community spaces: it's simply the choice of Social Leaders not to exercise that power, to be humble, and to rely on the community conferring different forms of authority.

Social Leadership is an extension of authority, from formal spaces into social ones: it's interesting because, in the Social Age, meaning is created largely in these spaces. They are the gateway to increased creativity and innovation: the lifeblood of agile organisations. We are not abandoning formal authority, but rather extending it, with a different set of skills.

The rise of the social CEO is an interesting phenomenon: people who exercise the ultimate positional authority and yet set it aside to engage directly with the community. Naturally our formal authority can carry across in terms of reputation to social spaces, but we can't rely on it. A celebrity may garner a large following from simply being famous: but if their input is inane, it won't grow, amplify or confer authority. Conversely, someone with no claim to fame as all can develop great authority purely in social spaces (through great storytelling and resonance).

Authority is complex, nuanced, contextual. In social terms, it's founded upon reputation (built in turn upon curation, storytelling, sharing and engagement in community). We can exercise both formal, hierarchical authority and also socially moderated authority, but one does not guarantee (or depend) upon the other. Overall, we exist in an ecosystem where formal authority is losing ground to the socially moderated variety, so understanding authority in terms of Social Leadership is powerful.

What does this mean:

1. Authority is founded upon reputation and it's within our power to generate socially moderated authority

2. Authority in social spaces is highly contextual and consensual, differing widely from formal authority. It's not power without limits, it's power through permission

3. Understanding amplification in social spaces is important to build authority and harks back to our work around 'curation' and 'storytelling'

How to develop this skill:

1. Develop consistent approaches to build authenticity and authority

2. Explore the nature of relationship and transactional engagement and focus on building more relationships

3. Learn how trust works in social spaces and reflect on how our actions impact on trust

3rd Dimension:
Technology Skill 7: Co-Creation in Social Leadership

Co-creation is about the ways we come together in social spaces to create meaning. It's a core Social Age process and we can see it everywhere. Collaborative technology enables us to co-create across wider spaces in synchronous, asynchronous and cross boundary ways. It allows us to form and grow communities and benefit from their sense making functions.

We achieve more together than we ever can alone. Social Learning spaces do not just bring us together to share what we have learnt, they bring us together to write a story together. To help understand the co-creative process, I've come up with a map of seven elements, seven ways that we use our social spaces to create meaning: building knowledge through iteration and reflection in a community.

These are the Seven Elements of Co-Creation: it's an exploration
of how we come together to create meaning.

In every village in medieval England was a tithe barn. The tithe was the percentage of the crop that went to the church and the tithe barn was where it was stored. As with all barns, it had two doors, the front ones very high, the back ones much lower. The fully laden carts came in the front, piled high, then left through the lower doors at the back, emptied. But the doors were not just to facilitate the passage of carts: with both doors thrown open, the space in the middle was breezy and is known as the threshing floor. The harvested wheat or corn was laid out and beaten with flails, to detach the grains from the heads. The resulting mass was scooped into woven pans, wide, like a scallop shell, and it was thrown into the air. The wind would catch the chaff, the fibrous husk that sits around the grains, and blow it out of the door, letting the grain itself fall back into the woven pan. Repeating this separated the wheat from the chaff.

Harvest and threshing were group activities, where everyone, from young to old, came together to carry out specific tasks. We use Social Learning spaces to refine our messages: to iterate our raw ideas into meaningful actions. To root out the wheat from the chaff. We do that by throwing our ideas into the wind and seeing what is left behind after the debate. It's how we refine our messages in these spaces. It's part of the co-creative process within the community.

Communities **share values**, it's what shapes them. If the values differ too far, the community fragments into new shapes. Shared value also sits at the heart of communication, we need to share value to understand each other and to develop more refined ideas. Socially collaborative spaces allow us to share value and encourage us to do so by letting us understand the value of other participants. Shared value fosters cooperation and lets us build progressively more complex constructs, based on the foundation values, knowledge and understanding. This is a co-creative process at work.

Part of refining our ideas and narratives in social spaces is that of **editing** things down. We can use social spaces in this function as we rehearse ideas. I've been writing about something called '*co-adaptation*' in music, it's about how two people adapt to match a beat. But my ideas are still raw, my stories unrefined, so I've been rehearsing and editing them all week in various social spaces (from LinkedIn to Yammer and the pub). Each time I tell the story, I get feedback and I refine what I say. The process of editing makes my narrative stronger. As my ideas reach maturity I should be able to edit them to the point that I can explain them concisely and with clarity. This only happens with careful editing and is central to the co-creative processes at play in Social Leadership.

I use a six step methodology for understanding how we learn. **Reflection** is a key but often neglected part. We need to take the learning and reflect upon it, to stand up the new learning against what we already know to be true and to develop our thinking accordingly. We may accept or reject new knowledge, but it's an active process that takes reflection. Why have I listed it as a co-creative process? Because reflection is not simply about sitting in a quiet room thinking about whether we believe in something or not. It's an active process that can be embedded in the community. I'm reflecting right now, sat in a cafe, sharing ideas with people through email, through Twitter, even through Facebook. These very ideas I'm sharing have dedicated time where I'm reflecting on what i'm going to say and I'm refining that message through (and with) my own social communities.

Social Leaders operate in multiple communities, in some of which they are a guest, others of which they may form and lead in more conventional senses: in all of them though, reflection is important, it's part of separating the wheat from the chaff.

Challenge is a vital part of the co-creative process: it's something that is done well, if constructively, in Social Learning and collaborative spaces. We can challenge ideas, argue our case and co-create a shared narrative out of it. The fact is that some of our ideas are strong, some weak, and appropriate challenge helps us to work out which is which. So challenge sits here as one of the seven ways that we use our social community spaces to co-create meaning, to learn, to lead.

Tempo has a role too: one of the ways to drive up engagement in change is to restrict the length of time that a community space is available, to give it a definite end. This helps drive up the tempo. We can view the range of social media across a spectrum from synchronous to asynchronous. Twitter or forum chatter is often nearly synchronous, virtually conversational. Blogs are more reflective and the shared narrative that we may document and build out of the space tends to be highly asynchronous. It's more broadcast than conversation. It's easy to lose momentum in learning or creative processes. Writing the books has taught me that: I have to dedicate time and share my learning with the community to maintain my own momentum, to get the job done. For those reasons, tempo, the ability to give us momentum and take conversations forward, is included as one of the seven co-creative elements.

Finally, **shared vision**. Not the vision of the individual, but rather the shared vision of the community. A desire to learn, to make a difference, a desire to share ideas and do something worthwhile. We come together in these spaces because of the vision, to be inspired by others, as well as to offer inspiration ourselves. It's also about our field of vision being wider with more eyes: more people bringing a wider range of experience, a wider range of sources, creating more wisdom and meaning. The breadth and differences within community make it stronger. Vision inspires us.

So, seven strands of co-creation, seven things we take from social spaces: *'refinement'*, *'shared value'*, *'editing'*, *'reflection'*, *'challenge'*, *'tempo'* and *'shared vision'*.

Technology enhances and helps narrate the co-creative process: the very permanence than can be problematic in certain circumstances is a benefit for others (particularly in support of knowledge management, building and capturing tribal knowledge and the iterative sense making in communities: as I write this I'm constantly referring back to primary conversations that happened on the blog.

In the midst of our reflection on the co-creative process, there's one thing that's well worth recognising: it's expressive. Artistic almost. Including co-creation within Social Leadership provides an opportunity to draw in our creative and expressive capabilities as well as our strategic and analytical ones. Just as Social Leadership crosses over from social to formal spaces, so too it crosses from analytical to creative ones.

Again, technology plays a role in this through it's ability to turn us into producers as well as consumers of content. Whilst formerly organisational communication was limited to PowerPoints and ClipArt, along with interminable emails and maybe a fax or two, today we communicate through many channels, collaborative shared workspaces, instant messaging and file sharing, using audio, video, mind mapping, drawing and knowledge management and productivity tools like EverNote and Paper by Fifty Three, which is the tool I use for all my illustrations.

What does this mean:

1. Co-creation takes place within our communities: it's a complex process of iteration and review

2. Co-creation relies on a foundation of trust and integrity: we can nurture the co-creative processes at work in our communities and, indeed, it's important that leaders do

3. It's a creative as much as technical process: we have to be tolerant of the debate and mistakes as we conduct our sense making activities

How do we develop these skills:

1. Explore the seven strands of co-creation: do you recognise them all in your work, or are you missing out?

2. Narrate examples of co-creation to better understand and reflect upon the process

3. Consider how trust is the foundation of co-creation and develop a plan to support your communities to have clarity of engagement

3rd Dimension:
Technology Skill 8: Social Capital in Social Leadership

With authority comes responsibility: or maybe responsibility drives a need for authority to enable us to do what's right. Social Capital can be defined as our ability to survive and thrive in online social spaces, but it's also about our responsibilities to safeguard others. Leadership in the Social Age is contextual, but always carries a responsibility to be inclusive. It is, after all, Social Leadership, founded within communities. I've become more worried recently that the very technology that permits and enhances collaboration draws ever wider the gap between the socially enabled and the disenfranchised: through poverty, relevance or cultural barriers.

As we've seen before, communities are based around shared values, shared responsibilities and sometimes a division of labour, but membership is not automatic: it requires certain social skills as well as the right opportunities. Without access to technology, it's hard to be a Social Leader. In societies where the views of minority groups are repressed or ignored, it's hard to build reputation and be part of a community. And forget about it just being minorities: where women are given fewer rights or lower status than men, or where they are prevented from collaborating widely and freely, we can't have effective Social Leadership.

Just as we've talked about the socially responsible business, so too we need to consider the social responsibility of the individual: a responsibility to seek out fairness, to act with humility, to support and promote the views of others and to develop the welfare of the community as a whole.

Social Leaders have high social capital themselves: they need to understand the foundations of the Social Age, the realities of the new social contract and the underlying technology. They also foster and develop this capability in others. They ensure nobody is excluded through design or by chance. A high moral imperative you might think, taking us into the realms of social justice, not leadership, but why would we aim any lower? There's no such thing as nearly equal: if we're not building inclusive communities, if we're not acting with humility, we're not living the values required to be Social Leaders.

Not that you have to be a saint: it's fine to be motivated by money, status or position, you just have to realise that this will exclude you from certain social forms of power (although it may, of course, reinforce other more conventional types).

We can view three elements within Social Capital for our purposes here: *'etiquette'*, *'humility'* and *'equality'*.

The first, **etiquette**, is, in some ways, the easiest: it's the simple rules of engagement and effectiveness in social collaborative spaces. This ranges from understanding the behaviours we use online (and how they differ from formal organisational spaces both because they're virtual but also because they're social/seml formal), through to understanding the functioning of things like hashtags and forums at a technical level.

Organisations need to consider actively developing these skills independently of specific projects: we can assume that people know how to access and participate in online communities if we like, but if we don't check, we neglect our responsibilities for inclusion and support. And the rules are complicated because they are not consistent: online social spaces can be complex, hostile, challenging or bemusing and often all four (they can, of course, be simple, supportive, enriching and engaging, but again, we can't assume this to be true).

Where communities are co-creative and sense making, we have to recognise that roles may be fluid: subject matter expertise may be fluid as well as the conversations develop. In the Social Age evolved relationships with knowledge, come down more to your ability to find things out than your actual knowledge of things.

Issues of identity and trust also become relevant: identity is more fluid in online spaces and can form a particular hazard as we become unable to compartmentalise conversations effectively if we don't understand who is in them. This compartmentalisation is important because we have to allow communities to form and become coherent in their function, which means building shared value and narrative power, all of which is built on a foundation of trust.

These are big areas to get into, and it's not necessarily the role of Social Leaders to train people, but they must understand the significance and be able to function themselves, to the point where they can diagnose that others are struggling.

Etiquette is about understanding how things work and being able to participate within social (and technical) conventions.

Humility is a mindset around collaboration and co-creation: it's a stance we take in community. It's about recognising the relevance of other views and being willing to set aside our own. Social Leaders are humble because their authority is contextual and consensual, granted by the whim and permission of the community. Social Leadership operates in seml formal spaces where formal hierarchies of power do not apply: it's not that we can't apply them, we can of course assert our formal authority, but that then changes the space into a formal one, not a social one, so the context is lost.

Humility allows us to share effectively: as long as we're prepared to be proven wrong. The point of co-creative spaces is to facilitate the creation of meaning relevant in the moment and the sharing of it through narrative. The point is not to impose our view or dominate the conversation: this would change the space from a collaborative one to a broadcast one, which is what many formal organisational channels become by default: they become about propagating formal organisational stories, not the narratives formed by communities. This ties in with how we organisationally take a stance on moderation and control: it's all very well allowing debate and discussion, but what do we do when we don't like what's said? Especially at times of change, this forms part of the role of Social Leadership, being humble enough to listen in social spaces when people may be disenfranchised or voiceless in formal ones.

Ultimately, I include humility in the model of Social Leadership because of my frustration with egocentric models and much of the training done around influencing and management, all of which assumes a foundation of formal power and authority for leaders that simply is being eroded in the Social Age. The role of the social leader is not one of control through exercise of positional authority: it's one of narrative magnetism, telling stories that are engaging and inclusive and draw us forwards and together.

Even as I write this I recognise the idealistic narrative I'm creating: but I believe it's true. To understand how social collaborative technologies allow us to cluster around magnetic ideas, to amplify and extend them, you only have to look at the viral memes that sweep through Facebook on a daily basis. Stories have power: they are magnetic and a form of leadership grounded in narrative and co-creation can draw upon that power.

Amplification isn't about brute force and older, broadcast, 'push' models: it's about engagement in depth, throughout multiple communities, about shaping narratives and sharing magnetic stories, filtering out the weaker ideas in our first reflective spaces, developing the stronger ones, curating, sharing. Amplification is a natural force we harness, but with humility: you can't achieve authority for Social Leadership through ego, you can only do it through consensus, within the right context.

The community can grant you the authority, but it can remove it too.

Equality is not something to strive for: it's something to fight for. Odd, maybe, that an act for Social Leaders should be to level the playing field and equalise, but it represents the fact that all voices need to be heard and respected equally.

If we just listen to the vocal or already empowered, we miss the wealth of wisdom and experience from the voiceless and hidden. Plus it assumes or imposes hierarchy in a space that strives for collaboration among equals.

Equality is not easy to achieve: in our shared global culture we experience different legal, ethical and cultural frameworks and we have to respect them, but it's still often clear what's right and what's wrong, and those are the things we have to fight for.

The trouble with fairness is that it doesn't fracture: it's slowly eroded. If we don't respect the people it's easy to respect, how can we hope to be tolerant across the wider gaps. If we don't challenge the laughter on the small things, how can we hope to tackle the really big ones? If equality doesn't start at home, how can we hope to expect it at work, or globally?

For an organisation to tolerate homophobia or racism, discrimination on the grounds of gender or belief is intolerable. It's wrong.

The culture is not broken because of one or two people in a remote location: it's broken because of the thirteen other people who laugh along because they don't dare to challenge the laughter. The culture is broken when one person feels like they're disenfranchised for being the one person who is right.

Social Capital is a big area and every time I revisit it, it gets bigger. But maybe that's because it's so important.

What does this mean:

1. Developing high social capital ourselves is about refining our skills whilst remaining humble

2. It's about drawing everyone together within communities and ensuring that we are fair in what we do and say

3. Individual social capital contributes to an organisation being fair, being equal

How do we build these skills:

1. The foundation skills of etiquette are mastered through practice and feedback

2. Humility is gained through reflection: through consistent action over time

3. Working with a mentor can help with both these things

4. Equality is about our mindset: exploring unconscious bias can be valuable, but it's also about constantly listening out for the voiceless and addressing disenfranchisement

3rd Dimension:
Technology Skill 9: Collaboration in Social Leadership

The NET Model of Social Leadership is a circle: the ideas and skills it contains live in constant beta, always being refined and adapted as the ecosystem evolves around us. It's not just technology that changes: social attitudes develop, legislation moves on, different voices become louder or less relevant, depending upon their ability to be agile. But, in as far as our journey has a start, a middle and an end (as every good story should), we have reached the final segment.

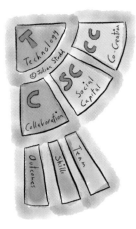

Collaboration sits at the end of 'Technology', the third Dimension of the NET Model and we can, to an extent, view it as the pinnacle of Leadership. Why? Let's explore:

Social Leaders start by defining their space, taking a stance, looking inwards and finding out what drives and motivates them and what they want to be known for. They learn how to refine their storytelling and communication skills around this core vision and then look to their communities to build reputation and authority. Along the way, they explore the purpose of those communities and their roles within them. Having done so, they seek to develop others, to safeguard them, to include them and ultimately to advance themselves, the organisations and their communities in line with best practice and what's right.

The ability to collaborate widely, to recognise the needs of individuals and organisations and to co-create communities and situations that can serve both is part of the purpose of Social Leadership.

In this sense, Collaboration is the peak: to be able to forge fair and productive relationships, to be able to 'make sense' of things, to create (and co-create) meaning and to effectively do that in an inclusive way that gets things done.

But the model is circular for a reason: because the Social Age is also about agility and fluidity: Social Leadership is consensual and contextual and we have to remain relevant. So, as we find our role and exercise our authority (through the permissions of the community), so we must revisit our stance and balance. Have we developed the right skills for today, but what skills will we need tomorrow? Are our communities strong enough, or do we need to enter, create or refine an existing one? Are our teams intact? Or do we need to develop, update or enhance them, either through development or addition (or indeed, removing someone).

Collaboration is about recognising validity in multiple viewpoints and being willing (and able) to account for them all. It's not about decision making through democratic process: you can still exercise strong and unilateral authority (recognising that it's permissive authority).

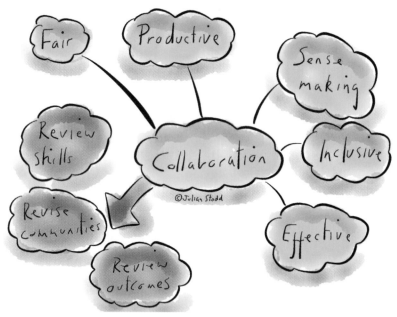

Collaboration is a complex process: it's about being fair and productive.
It's about sense making, being inclusive, becoming effective.

Social Leaders should seek to be fair: to do what's right, not just what's covered by process or law. It's about rebalancing the relationship between organisations and individuals to include fairness, a recognition that the needs of both can be reconciled if we are careful. This fairness leads to the ability to better form and participate within communities, communities which make us effective. Because neither membership nor authority is assured, we have to build our own foundations for this, and fairness is a good place to start.

Collaboration is about being productive: productive through being able to get things done, to instigate and carry through change, through collaboratively owned and driven change. It's the co-created and co-owned nature of the Social Age change communities that makes them effective.

We can focus on three elements of collaboration: 'Team', 'Skills' and 'Outcomes'.

'Team' is about how Social Leadership, which operates in seml formal spaces, bridging between the fully formal and entirely social, relates to traditional team structures.

We've explored widely how Social Leaders curate reputation and operate within communities, where their power is consensual, but they also operate within formal teams and often have formal responsibilities to those teams (which may be in conflict with those of their communities). This is the tightrope that Social Leaders have to tread, forever with one foot in the realms of formal hierarchy and authority. It may not always be easy.

Within their formal teams, Social Leaders also conduct sense making activities

Engagement in social spaces is highly sensitive to trust: but the types of trust invested in formal hierarchies may be different. Within a formal context, we take it as read that a manager or leader may know things about our circumstances that they can't share with us. In social circles, if a friend withheld information about our wellbeing, we would lose trust. As leaders venture out of the purely formal and into social, they start to confront these issues.

Social Leadership is still a semI formal style: it's not devolved from responsibility and regulation. It's a matter of understanding where the challenges lie and approaching them with integrity and clarity.

There's a responsibility on individuals too: we have to accept that information may still be segregated, that Social Leadership approaches are informal but still may cross into certain hierarchies. As I said earlier: it's a balance between how social approaches can complement and reinforce formal ones.

The mindset of collaborating with our teams rather than leading them through formal authority may be new: it's a magnetic approach to leadership.

We need new skills to collaborate effectively: we've already covered eight of them here, and these skills need to be mastered over time, refined and shared. Under the purview of social capital, it's not about learning skills to differentiate us from the crowd: it's about learning skills to share them with the crowd. Old notions of keeping our knowledge hidden away cease to apply in the Social Age: sharing is a differentiating skill and one that we should have mastered by this point, and that applies to skills as well as knowledge.

As we complete our reflection on collaboration, we have to consider outcomes: how effective have we been? Our value depends upon our ability to be more effective, to create meaning and get things done. Collaboration is the platform upon which we can deliver that effectiveness, creating a magnetic leadership approach and co-creating change within our communities and teams, both formal and social.

We can use our new skills around narrative and storytelling to ensure that our success is shared internally, back into formal spaces, as well as socially. It's all part of closing the circle, ensuring that people accompany us on our journey and it supports the ongoing reputation economy we operate in.

With that in mind, part of our collaborative efforts have to be about reinforcing and growing the reputation and authority of others: by saying thank you, sharing reflections, writing reviews, making recommendations, giving feedback, offering mentoring, coaching others, sharing insights, a continuous process of feeding the community and drawing upon it's skills.

What does it mean:

1. Collaboration involves negotiating the space between competing needs and desires of individuals and organisations

2. The win is to compromise but to be highly effective

3. Humility may be our greatest strength

4. We must share outcomes and reflect on our approach, strengths and weaknesses

5. We need to do so whilst supporting the ongoing development of our teams

How do we build these skills:

1. We need to address models of negotiation and compromise, developing our skills in these areas

2. We have to rehearse our narratives of success: how are we building the reputation of others?

3. We must circle around the model to review our other core skills and ensure they stay up to date

Part 3: Application

Part 3: Application

Now that we've explored the Foundations of the Social Age and taken a trip through the NET Model of Social Leadership, the third section of this book is about application. It's based around a series of posts from my Blog on various applications and contexts for Social Leadership, with some additional commentary added.

Why social businesses, leaders and learners need to understand amplification

I was never much good at organised games at school. To be honest, I just wasn't very engaged. Whilst the other boys were charging around the rugby pitch in the rain, sliding through the mud and acquiring scars to carry with pride, I was apt to be daydreaming at the back, looking at the trees or pondering why the ball was an odd shape.

'Stoneface' Stoneham, the games master, had one strategy to deal with this: shouting. He was not a subtle man, more used to motivation by volume than leadership by consensus, and certainly not a man to stare and trees or ponder the meaning of ellipsoids. Not unless it would help you kick it over the goal line anyway.

So Stoneface would stand there bellowing at me and I'd stand there in my wet socks with mud up my legs pondering life, whilst we both failed to comprehend each other until it dawned on me that shouting ever more loudly will probably not get you far in life.

And anyway, why shout loudly when all you really need to do is be amplified by others?

Amplification is the secret heart of social: it's what makes memes travel around the world, what makes adverts go viral, it's what gives good ideas a life of their own and ensures that bad ones sink. Amplification is what everyone wants, what everyone needs, but only a few can get.

Except old Stoneface of course. I think he shouted because he was just unhappy. I'd have been unhappy dealing with my ten year old self too.

Understanding amplification is important, because not everyone amplifies your messages. In fact, hardly anyone amplifies, and a tiny percentage of those who do will be relevant for your particular messages, because amplification is contextual: different people amplify different things. Social Leaders need to understand how their vision is amplified, social businesses need to understand the perils of amplification, social learners need to identify strong amplifiers and include them in their personal learning networks.

The Social Age is tied up in networks: connected individuals, each of whom in turn is connected out to others. It's a tangled web we weave and it's changing every minute of the day.

Building and curating the shape and structure of your network is important, as is your ability to shape and structure your messages to encourage amplification. Because everyone curates the content they share, to a greater or lesser extent, we can start to differentiate between those who add value to everything that passes them by, and those who simply recycle content. We can start to see those who are discerning in their messages and those who simply aren't.

In the democratised age of publishing, everyone can publish, but we have lost the editorial role. Well, to a large extent, this role is picked up by the community, particularly the amplifiers. People who are discerning of what they see, as well as active in amplifying that which they like, act as the first line editors of social content.

Whenever either we (or organisations within the social marketplace) broadcast anything to our communities, some people consume (and leave it at that), whilst others amplify. The amplifiers may be shouting into empty space (if they are not well connected or have a low reputation for amplifying without discernment) or they may be speaking to the converted, preaching to a crowd that is hungry for more.

The great thing about connecting with amplifiers who have a strong reputation is that they have themselves curated a focused community: in theory, you can get a higher hit rate within those focussed communities than you can directly to the whole world.

In the Social Age, those people who are more adept at engaging with the amplifiers, and who curate a strong reputation for adding value to what they amplify, will be more influential, have a greater ability to build reputation. Organisations need to understand that this will not just happen through their formal channels, but through the informal ones too: people who sit entirely outside formal hierarchies of power and authority may curate strong reputations and build influence, entirely subverting formal structures. This can scare people significantly.

When messages are amplified within a community, they tend to gain momentum. The greater the amplification, the greater the momentum, especially when every discerning amplifier projects your messaging into ever more refined communities, who may share interests and be more amenable to what you have to say.

Eventually all but the most engaging messages will die out, but you can certainly influence how far your messages get, by crafting them well and curating a strong first line network. By being an effective amplifier yourself and by engaging with others, by building your own reputation and facilitating others to build theirs.

Getting a good grasp on amplification and momentum, much as getting a good grasp on a slippery, mud covered rugby ball, will get you far in the game.

Today's blog is adapted from the writing I'm doing this week on my new book: 'learning and working in the Social Age'.

Becoming a Social Leader: organisational strategies for engaging and retaining talent

To face the challenges of the Social Age, a time when change is constant and innovation and creativity key for survival, organisations need Social Leadership. Social Leaders will enable them to develop and maintain their agility, their ability to respond to change, to innovate and be creative, to survive. They need people who are fluent in the technology and social conventions that enable the formation of communities and the engagement of those communities with the everyday challenges of the business.

But Social Leaders may not arrive through traditional development channels. They may emerge from within or need to be attracted from outside the business. Social Leaders may not be identified or developed through existing success planning efforts.

From an organisational perspective, we have to recognise that, as we move ever further away from the concept of 'jobs for life', we can no longer expect to have a monopoly on leadership development. People are owning their own careers, outside the formal hierarchies of positional power and authority, which are, in any case, crumbling under the agility and effectiveness of more social models. We need strategies to attract great candidates from outside the organisation, and we need a curriculum to develop Social Leadership internally.

Social Leaders are founded more on their ability to create meaning than their pure knowledge, something that we need to keep in mind when we go looking for them. Whilst historically the organisation has used formal training as a chance to impart both knowledge and skills, today it's worth thinking more about providing mentoring and challenge.

Knowledge itself is easy to come by, and skills are forged in the fires of practice, the reality of constant change and deadline driven projects. What is harder to come by are great mentors and appropriate challenge, so by providing this and organisation can become magnetic to talent (both internally, to retain emergent Social Leaders, and externally to attract them).

In the Social Age we see that people are more attracted to formally recognised qualifications, so simply saying we run an 18 month leadership programme for top talent may be less effective than saying we provide internal and external mentors (and support your time to work with them), we provide dedicated spaces for challenge (internally for cohorts and with external expertise bought in for specific units) and that we support you eventually pursuing an external qualification (recognising that nobody will be here forever and that transferrable qualifications are meaningful).

Social Leaders can be recognised by having a strong reputation: they will be active in communities and able to use that engagement to be more effective, individually and within teams. It's a trait of Social Leaders that they don't just develop their own skills, they have the humility and foresight to develop others, recognising that teams are stronger than individuals.

In the diagram above you'll see that the foundations of Social Leadership are supported by a network of mentors, people who help emergent Social Leaders to define the spaces to work in and moderate their actions with the experience of others. Once the foundations are in place, and reputation is building, it's community and knowledge management that are key. Fluidity of role within community is important: because social leaders don't rely on positional authority, often they are not in a leadership role at all, and certainly there is no assumption that they will be.

Knowledge management is important because Social Leaders are islands in the sea of dross that flows through official communication channels. They filter and sort, adding value to anything they pass on. Contextualising information and making it relevant to audience, as well as using data driven conversations to influence and support.

Authority is not the end point of Social Leadership: it's a by product of the activities that make a leader. If you are agile, if you are supported by appropriate mentors and engaged within communities (in fluid roles, adding value), if your approach to knowledge management is strong and you contextualise knowledge appropriately, then your authority will grow.

For organisations, the challenge is twofold: firstly, to recognise that the existing, formal hierarchies, are changing, that the leadership models of the twentieth century Knowledge and Manufacturing ages may not suit the twenty first century Social Age, secondly to recognise that we don't forge Social Leaders through courses and accreditation, we do it through mentoring, reward and the creation of spaces for talent to thrive.

Whilst the very nature of work is adapting to the realities of life today, whilst we see increasing focus on ethical business and collaborative working, there has never been a better time to assess your stance on Social Leadership.

The Social Age needs Social Leaders. Some of these will be grown from within, some attracted from outside, but whatever the case, we need to develop skills for narrative and engagement, facilitated by technology.

The Social Business: aligning Social Learning and Leadership to the values driven organisation

There's a shift towards a more social culture of business: not just engaged in social spaces, but values driven and responsible. Being proud of your credentials is no longer the preserve of niche cosmetics manufacturers and cooperatives: it's now on the mainstream agenda of many global organisations.

Values driven? It's about deeds, not just words. It's about a social contract between employer and employee, about recognising that in the Social Age this relationship may be impermanent, but it can persist over time through different iterations. Employed, in community, freelance. Organisations no longer exist in splendid isolation, but rather within an ecosystem of associates and a community of brand. Their reputation is forged in this space: by their leaders, their teams, their competition and the wider community of consumers.

So you need to be engaged: as an organisation you need to be engaged in a responsible way with an authentic tone of voice in the social spaces that surround you. As an individual, you need to curate your reputation (to use the principles of NET) and as a leader you need to facilitate the relationship between the two.

Social Learning and Social Leadership come together to support the values driven business, because the narrative of the business has to be co-created and co-owned by the teams and communities. In the Social Age, brand is a collaboratively defined experience, not solely owned by the organisation, so only authentic engagement with community will allow the building of a social brand.

Learning needs to be broader and wider than previously thought: it's about engagement over time, about supporting the holistic development of the individual, so not just needs driven and planned learning, but also learning driven by curiosity or forged within communities.

I believe that the values driven business, a business that is responsible and engaged, can only be grown by the organisation if it finds and develops a Social Leadership model and enhances it's formal learning interventions with Social Learning spaces. It's a social model of learning to deliver the social business.

Social Leadership:
Communities and meaning

We don't just belong to one community: in the Social Age, we belong to many. Maybe there was a time when we all lived in caves and gathered around campfires to skin mammoths, when we were constrained by being in just one tribal group, but today our membership is wide and varied. Some are social groupings, based around old university friends, school mates, chess clubs or gardening, whilst others based around our offices at work, some around specific interests (like car mechanics or yoga) and others around individual projects.

Sometimes our interactions with these groups are just for fun, whilst at other times they are focused around problem solving for specific challenges.

We interact within communities to create meaning, in the moment. That's what the Social Age is all about: moving beyond pure knowledge to finding the meaning and taking transformative action.

Social Leaders understand this. They take facts, previous experience and knowledge and share this, within their communities, to create meaning: they curate and interpret this information and make it specific to the audiences that they share it with. This act of curation and sharing builds their reputation, and reputation subverts more formal models of authority. And if there isn't a community there to do this in, they form one for the duration of the project (they have the social capital to form and develop these).

The challenge for organisations is this: they need to identify and cultivate Social Leadership skills, whilst at the same time being magnetic to new talent. They need to create and tolerate the socially collaborative spaces that these communities need, both from a technological and moderation perspective. You need to be seen as a creative and innovative place to work, a true Social Age business with a mindset and policies to prove it.

Today, agile social workers, innovative Social Leaders have choices: they can work for you or they can work elsewhere. Where do you want them to turn? Can you afford to lose them?

Not all relationships are equal

Relationships come in all shapes and sizes, but not all are equal. We form communities around a wide variety of subject and needs, some based on shared values, some on reciprocal exchange, some formed around contracts, some on shared hope, but the foundations affect the nature of interactions and ways that those communities respond to change.

Social Leaders need to ability to engage within multiple communities and to form spontaneously emergent ones around specific challenges. Social Learners need to engage effectively within communities to form consensus and develop learning narratives. Communities develop momentum for change and act as first line support as it unfolds. It's worth us understanding how relationships are formed within them and what their foundations look like so that we are better able to nurture them.

There needs to be an element of trust within relationships, but it's naive to think that this means 'trust' without conditions: look at the type of relationship we have with our banks or insurance companies. We 'trust' them without money, but only within a framework of regulation. We trust them because there is a mechanism to deal with failures of trust.

Relationships may rely on blind faith, founded upon reputation, or may include shared goals and values: there may be an expectation of reciprocity, but equally a relationship may be altruistic or based purely upon monetary reward with no expectation of anything else in return.

Why every business needs Social Leaders

Social Leadership is a style of leadership the fosters innovation and creativity, collaboration and effectiveness. It does this by focussing on nine components that, together, develop the mindset and skills required to build reputation and authority in the Social Age. It's founded on a belief that the ecosystem we live in is changing: that our relationship with knowledge has evolved, that your value is no longer founded on what you know, but rather on your ability to create meaning, your ability to function in formal and informal networks to create momentum and support and sustain change. Social Leaders are collaborative and tell powerful stories.

In other words, 'fit for purpose' no longer means getting trained up and then operating on a level playing field until your next promotion: the agile learner and the agile business both need to develop and rehearse the skills required in a world in constant change.

Why do we need agility? Because process and control will not deliver the space for reflection and experimentation that is needed to be excellent. Agility is about iteration and feedback, it's about co-creation and collaboration. It's about a culture that supports learning from mistakes and that tells stories of it's success.

Social Leaders will be both found and grown within the business, but also need to be identified and attracted from outside. A business that supports social ways of working will be magnetic to this type of talent, and when you're magnetic, it makes life much easier!

Social Leadership is based around three core areas: Narrative is about curating your space and telling effective stories, Engagement is about creating and sustaining communities and Technology is about momentum and the co-creation of meaning.

The formal networks and hierarchies that defined the business of the past are being swept away by changing dynamics of power, knowledge and authority. People build reputation within communities, based upon their ability to curate appropriate content, create strong narratives, share these appropriately and support others in the co-creation of meaning from these stories. Businesses need to be able to engage in these seml formal and informal spaces, as well as still retaining credibility in formal ones. We see time and again instances where businesses believe that this is simply about social media policies and having a Facebook page, but it's far, far beyond that.

When we build a population of engaged leaders who able to lead in socially collaborative ways, we build the foundations of agility and creativity that will sustain the organisation into the future. Engaged with both it's employees, leaders and communities.

Creating and sharing: why we are all curators in the Social Age

I read a study this morning from the Pew Research Centre's Internet Project. They interviewed a thousand American adults on their internet habits: 54% of them had posted original photos or videos to websites and 47% shared content they found elsewhere.

Sharing and curating are habits of the Social Age, they're deeply embedded in how we interact online. In my Social Leadership model, I explore how we curate this content, how we tell stories about it and how we share it effectively, but one thing should be clear: it's not a minority of people that do this. The curators are everywhere. To differentiate ourselves, to build reputation, we just have to do it well.

Effective sharing is about adding context, about interpretation, about storytelling. It's what makes something relevant to you when it's of no interest to me. Sharing is about quality not volume. It's about timelines not randomness.

Organisations need to adapt to the realities of the Social Age: using enabling technologies to let people share effectively, building storytelling capability and forming strong and dynamic communities.

The reputation of Social Leaders

Reputation is forged in our communities, founded up upon our actions, our choices, our stance. It's about our ability to curate great content, add layers of context and share it effectively, to be known as someone who gets things done and does that collaboratively and whilst developing others. In the Social Age, reputation forms a bedrock of leadership and isn't hierarchical or bestowed by others. It's earned through actions and deeds.

Many leadership development activities focus on behaviours and skills, but miss the broader picture: leadership is curated. We make active choices what ethical and behavioural stances we will take on any subject. We choose who to bring into our networks and who to exclude, who to develop and who to avoid. Our choices around community building are not accidental, they are considered.

To effectively develop Social Leaders, we need to support them building their reputation, by teaching the concepts of curation, narration and storytelling.

Our reputation is highly portable: it comes with us wherever we go and into whatever communities we engage with, so it's worth exerting some effort to get it right.

Social Leadership resides with individuals: whilst older forms of positional or subject based authority were dependent upon longevity, Social Leadership and reputation can bypass all of these.

The challenge for organisations is this: how do you support your leaders in building their reputation? It needs investment in socially collaborative technologies, in training for the core skills of curation and storytelling, and in a mindset that recognises the evolving nature of work.

Organisations that get this right will be truly agile, able to benefit from the creativity and agility that Social Leadership brings.

How Social Leaders fight fires wisely

A busy day today, supporting a team under pressure. I recognise in myself some patterns of behaviour: some of them constructive, others less so. It turns out I'm far from perfect under pressure, but am, at least, in good company.

So today the blog is late, it's evening and I'm sat in an office, thinking about dinner. I'm hungry, but the wanted to share some thoughts on how Social Leaders fight fires.

The premise of Social Leaders is to be agile, to create meaning in the moment and to do it again, differently, tomorrow. So when better to do this than under pressure? Social Leaders work in communities: they collaborate and co-create solutions. They don't rely on hierarchical authority, but instead build consensus in communities and communicate effectively. They recognise patterns, both in themselves and others, but work to build out of that, providing support and acting with humility.

In the Social Age, we leave nobody alone: we recognise that responsibility is shared and that we are stronger when we acknowledge our weaknesses. Ego has a limited role in a highly functioning team. That doesn't mean we can't build our reputation, but it has to be based on the nine core principles of Social Leadership: we curate our position, we tell effective stories and share them wisely. We operate in communities, build our reputation and develop our authority based upon that. We co-create meaning, build the social capital of others (whilst supporting them with humility) and collaborate effectively.

And at the end of the day, the only fires we recognise are the ones we sit around to share our stories, to build our team community and learn together. This is not an ideal notion: if we are wise, we learn to fight fires effectively. Wisdom trumps stubbornness and dogma every time.

A note on Curation

The difference between my attic and the British Museum is that one is curated, whilst the other is full of junk. To be fair on the British Museum, they've got a lot more stuff than me to sort out...

Curation is partly the sciences of organisation and conservation and partly the art of interpretation and storytelling. In the Social Age, it's also part of the art of leadership.

Curation is about choosing your stage and gathering together the skills and capabilities that you need to perform.

In the NET Model of Social Leadership, I use 'curation' as the first component, because it's the foundation for everything else: curate your space and then develop the stories you can tell from it.

Curation is a skill in it's own right, and an agile one at that: just as the BM changes it's displays over time, so too we need to adapt and bring on new scenery, new skills, new tools. A museum that doesn't curate itself well becomes dusty and irrelevant: a risk that faces us all.

Great museums (and the British Museum is a truly great museum) find a stance that is informative, engaging, educational and challenging. Something we could all usefully emulate.

Social engagement and exclusion

There's a competitive advantage to being connected: communities form around common interests and needs and the price of membership is always balanced or exceeded by the benefits it brings. In communities, we can produce more, distribute fairly, provide support and care, have strength in numbers and shape the world to suit our needs. Whilst yesterdays communities were anchored in coal mines and sources of minerals, today we have just as many centred on subject matters, common goals and shared needs. Our online communities are many and varied.

For leaders, social engagement is essential: the premise of Social Leadership is that we create meaning, we build reputation and hence authority through our communities. Whilst this socially moderated power does not always replace formal authorities, (although it may fully subvert them), it's certainly important and may be the difference between success in any given role and failure.

For society, social engagement brings benefits and perils: the benefit, that it's easier to rally to a cause, be it fracking or immigration, human rights or X Factor. The peril? That we may inadvertently create chasms of opportunity between the 'haves' and 'have nots', separated not only by access to technology, but also by lack of social capital and even freedoms to participate.

So every action to create and share should be accompanied by an awareness of the hidden society, the disenfranchised and voiceless. Social Leadership includes a responsibility to form communities, to reach out and counter the forces that separate and divide.

Socially engaged leaders and workers are pioneering new approaches to 'working out loud', sharing their iterative thought processes and the inner workings of their personal narratives. This approach, within a supportive community, is powerful and rewarding, relieving us of the fear of mistakes and supporting us to emulate all of part of a particular journey. But for the disenfranchised, especially those who are powerless through institutional convention or coercion, culture or law (for example, societies where women are discouraged or forbidden to contribute), such freedoms are a long way off. The gap between the socially engaged free elements of our global society and the socially repressed or disenfranchised may be growing wider.

Social collaborative technology breaks down barriers: geographies no longer divide us, language may not separate us as instantaneous translation comes ever closer, knowledge is no longer hidden away but rather served up to us on smartphones and tablets and parsed into ever more digestible chunks. We no longer need a printing press to make a statement and no longer need a TV station to broadcast it. We are empowered by technology to learn, to form opinions, to craft our stories and share them widely. Or at least we are if we are socially engaged.

In my optimistic moments, I see that this engagement is pervasive and has great momentum: I doubt that even the most oppressive regimes can block access forever, but maybe at a more local level we miss the problems. Within our own organisations, what forces prevent membership? Do we discriminate on grounds of age, of grammar, of department? Do our policies on social media and privacy prevent sharing and the formation of opinions, or encourage it.

Changes in communication technology drive changes in wider society: our ability to form and belong to communities changes how we live and work. These impacts are felt at a micro and macro level. On a personal and local basis, our social relationships are transformed by social networking sites that expand and enhance our ability to maintain a volume of loose social ties, whilst at a macro level our freedoms to challenge authority are enhanced by the ways that ideas permeate and turn viral. Wikileaks would not have happened without a raft of underlying technologies and changes in our relationship with knowledge.

The Social Age is facilitated by technology, but formed on an understanding that engagement will be free and unhindered. Where access is prevented, by convention or law, through coercion or poverty, opportunities are lost and people get left behind.

A note on 'humility' in Social Leadership

The Social Age is about creating meaning within communities: but it's not about the cult of personality. It's not about owning these spaces or influencing others. It's not about the loudest voice, but rather about an ability to learn, about a fluidity of role, about humility to learn from others and contribute when you can add value.

Social Leaders need to be humble, to share widely and be generous without expectation of reciprocity. The Social Age is reputation based, not transactional.

Your magnetism in the Social Age will come from the space you curate, from the wisdom with which you tell your stories and how effectively you share them. It will be founded in humility.

Social Leadership is an approach to leadership that recognises and reflects the realities of the Social Age. It's based on reputation, forged in communities and fuelled by generosity, sharing, humility and collaboration.

Social Leadership is contextual and of it's time: our time. The walls that surrounded us have become permeable: our communities span the globe and stay with us throughout our careers. The skills to survive and thrive in the Social Age have evolved, covering Narrative, Engagement and Technology, and will continue to evolve as the ecosystem and driving forces change. Social Leaders are agile and can keep up: they surf the waves of change and relish the fact that change is the new constant.

I see Social Leadership (and it's associated elements around co-created change and community management) as forming pillars of my professional practice for years to come. We live and work in the Social Age, where only organisations and individuals who are agile will survive and thrive, and where we can't leave anyone behind.

Summary

The journey towards Social Leadership takes us through nine stages: we CURATE our space, choosing the stage we will perform from. We develop our STORYTELLING skills, learning how to structure the narrative and tell stories that are relevant and timely, interpreting the world around us to create meaning. We SHARE those stories wisely.

Social Leaders work around Engagement to build their REPUTATION, founded upon their stories and shared in COMMUNITIES, where they actively participate in the discussion. Their AUTHORITY is based upon their reputation, not hierarchy or position.

Social Leaders recognise the facilitating power of Technology and have high SOCIAL CAPITAL, as well as actively developing that in others. They CO-CREATE meaning, recognising that the process of consulting and participating in community makes them stronger and they COLLABORATE widely, with humility, with no expectation of reciprocity.

Social Leaders are agile, fit for the Social Age. These are skills that we can develop, but they're based on recognising that the fundamental nature of work and learning is changing. We have to master the Foundation of the Social Age to be true Social Leaders.

Postscript: The Future of Leadership

I wrote this short article in 2014, which proved a big hit on SlideShare, so I'm including it as an endnote, summarising the landscape we've navigated in this book.

We live in the Social Age, where formal models of authority and power are being subverted by more socially moderated relationships, where reputation is key. As organisations see innovation and creativity as key to agility, they persist in mitigating against their own success through an over reliance on process and attempts to control technology. They fail in the gap between process and excellence. Innovation and creativity can only thrive in environments that are inclusive, that develop trust, that are fair.

Our ecosystem is changing: a new social contract and changed nature of work, the widespread adoption of socially collaborative technology, an evolution of our relationship with knowledge and the rise of the Socially Responsible Business, one that recognises how attitudes to equality and fairness equate to shareholder value and agility.

Agility: the ability to respond, to flex, to find the meaning and execute a solution. That's what sits at the heart of Social Leadership. Knowing things used to be enough, but no more: in an age where technology brings simple knowledge to our fingertips, it's our ability to work within and alongside our communities to create meaning that counts. Communities are *'sense making'* entities: providing us with challenge and support, access to expertise and an ability to circumvent hierarchy, but our role in these communities is fluid. Social Leadership is contextual.

The nature of work is changing: less about what happens within the four walls of the office, more about your reputation within communities. Reputation that will get you this job and help you find the next. Reputation that will make you an effective Social Leader by allowing you to draw upon the power of your communities, to create meaning, to share stories widely and wisely.

The Social Age requires Social Leaders: leaders who work within and alongside communities to create meaning, to deliver. They are able to operate both within the formal environments and the seml formal spaces that surround it. We view this in three Dimensions: **Narrative**, **Engagement** and **Technology**.

The first concept of social leadership is '**Narrative**': this is about curation, storytelling and sharing. About finding things out, finding the meaning in it and sharing it with relevant people, adding value as you do so. It's about being part of the conversation instead of part of the noise. Whilst socially collaborative technologies allow us to share easily, so much of what is shared, copied and re-blogged is simply noise. Social Leaders cut through the noise with relevance and clarity.

So Narrative is about:

CURATION – finding things out and determining what's valid from what's just noise. It's about identifying networks and communities and seeing where the nodes and amplifiers sit. It's about quality and coherence, not volume and mass.

STORYTELLING – do you know how to identify the narrative that sits under the story? Can you find the meaning? Social Leaders need to be able to take their curated ideas and knowledge and forge coherent narratives, then flesh them out into stories that are relevant and timely to the audience. It's about understanding how stories are told and retold, so although the individual words change, the narrative is constant.

SHARING – this is a core skill of the Social Age. Curating content, finding the meaning and then sharing the stories effectively. This may involve technology, but it's not purely that. It's a mindset to share that counts: recognising that knowledge in itself is no longer enough.

In summary, Narrative is about curating knowledge, finding the meaning within it, forming stories and understanding how to share and amplify these. Narrative skills form the heart of personal effectiveness for Social Leaders.

Following on from Narrative is '***Engagement***'. Engagement is about:

COMMUNITY – social leaders operate in communities: both formal and informal spaces where meaning is created. With narrative, we looked at how to be an effective storyteller, with engagement we are looking at the spaces those stories are told in and how to use them to build your reputation and authority. Community is about understanding why people engage in communities and how we can both form and sustain them effectively.

REPUTATION – as we move beyond purely hierarchical forms of power and authority, we enter the reputation economy. Reputation forms the engine of our effectiveness. If our reputation is weak, even if our stories are strong, we will struggle to get them heard or amplified. Reputation is forged in communities, founded on the quality of our stories and effectiveness of our sharing.

AUTHORITY is born from reputation, based on the stories we curate. Authority in the social age is fluid, not fixed in bricks and mortar, and may be contextual. This component of Social Leadership is about recognising when authority is exercised and how, about becoming magnetic.

In summary, Engagement is about understanding the shape and structure of informal and formal communities, understanding how and why people come together to work and learn. Reputation is the engine that powers our effectiveness: it's based on actions, not hierarchy, and authority is the outcome. We seek authority as leaders, but it's based on everything we've seen so far: curating knowledge, finding meaning, telling stories and understanding the ecosystem they exist in.

Following Engagement comes '***Technology***'. This isn't about circuit boards and operating systems, it's about social collaboration and reach.

CO-CREATION is the process by which meaning is created within communities and the way in which culture changes over time. I use a seven stage model of co-creation, often taking place within scaffolded Social Learning environments. Co-creation and the co-ownership of change are core concepts for the Social Age. Relevant to this are notions of the three levels of narrative: personal, co-created in groups and organisational.

SOCIAL CAPITAL is one's ability to survive and thrive in these spaces. Effective social leaders have high social capital and develop it in others. This generosity and humility reinforces reputation and authority.

COLLABORATION is what it's all about: coming together and creating meaning, beyond that which we can do alone. Social Leaders collaborate widely: they engage in relationships without an expectation of immediate reciprocity. In time, all things balance out.

In summary, Technology is about socially collaborative conversations, about the co-creation of meaning in communities, about supporting engagement and development in these communities and about collaborating, to achieve more than we ever can alone.

Leadership is changing: we need to adapt our view of how we attract and retain effective leaders. We need a model of talent magnetism.

About Julian

I'm a writer and commentator on learning, leadership, creativity, culture and change. I write a blog every day at www.julianstodd.wordpress.com

I guess my work is about how people learn, how they adapt, about creativity and agility, about being effective and curious.

I work with global organisations who are interested in something new. I help them find a way.

I write about the Social Age: a time when the nature of work has evolved, when social collaborative technology is changing how we interact, where the socially responsible business is on the rise and where reputation and authority built in social spaces subverts formal hierarchies and systems.

I am founder and Captain of SeaSalt Learning and BlackBeard eLearning.

SeaSalt Learning is a global change consultancy that helps organisations adapt to change. Our programmes are around Social Leadership and learning, culture, creativity, innovation and learning technology. www.SeaSaltLearning.com

BlackBeard Digital is our eLearning and media production studio www.WeAreBlackBeard.com

I present widely at workshops, conferences and webinars. You can find me easily online or follow me on Twitter for details @julianstodd

Previous Books by Julian Stodd

"Exploring the World of Social Learning"

"Mindset for Mobile Learning - a journey through theory and practice"

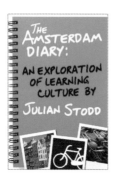

"Amsterdam Diary - an exploration of learning culture"

"Learning, Knowledge and Meaning - the Singapore Diary"

"Julian Stodd's Learning Methodology - designing effective eLearning"

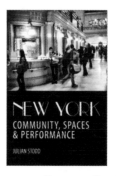

"New York - community, spaces & performance"